A
Transgender's
Faith

Walt Heyer

Copyright ©2015 Walt Heyer

A Transgender's Faith by Walt Heyer

ISBN: 978-1506155357
First printed in 2006 under the title *Trading My Sorrows*

All rights reserved solely by the author. The author guarantees all contents are original and do not infringe on the legal rights of any other person or work. No part of this publication may be reproduced or transmitted in any form or by any means without written permission of the author.

Unless otherwise indicated, Bible quotations are taken from:

THE MESSAGE. Copyright (c) 1993, 1994, 1995, 1996, 2000, 2001, 2002. Used by permission of NavPress Publishing Group and
The New American Standard Bible˙, Copyright © 1960, 1962, 1963, 1968, 1971, 1972, 1973, 1975, 1977, 1995 by The Lockman Foundation Used by permission." (www.Lockman.org)

Contact the author:
WaltsBook@yahoo.com

Website:
www.SexChangeRegret.com

Dedication

To all who gave so much so often for so long, shining through the darkness. Your love, your tears and your prayers proved more powerful than the torment and confusion in me.

To the many I hurt so much so often and for so long. I pray for your forgiveness and I pray healing will come for you by knowing the truth.

To my wonderful wife, my editor and collaborator. Without you, publishing would not have been possible. Thank you, my love, for a truly great job.

To Jesus Christ, my lord and savior. What a blessing it is to be the vessel you used to bring this story to life.

"I'm so grateful to Christ Jesus for making me adequate to do this work... Grace mixed with faith and love poured over me and into me. And all because of Jesus."
1 Timothy 1:12,14
The Message Bible

Foreword

In 1972, I met Walt when he brought his family to Forest Home Conference Center. A friendship started that has lasted, though broken and bumpy, for these thirty-four years.

In 1980, when Walt was promoted to national port operations manger for the Honda Motor Corporation, we celebrated. In 1981, when I heard the news about Walt, I was shocked. Walt had recklessly and senselessly sunk into a wayward, abhorrent lifestyle that cost him his marriage, his family and his career.

For the next three years we kept in touch regularly. I prayed, cared, threatened and wept over his squandered choices and his distraught family. Then Walt left the area and we had no more contact until 2003 when my wife, Carol and I walked into the church in Southern California, where I was scheduled to preach.

For almost fifty years I have believed and preached the grace and mercy of God, and that day I was privileged to see a miracle—living proof—of that divine grace, when I again saw Walt and met his wife, Kaycee.

This book is a true story of deception, love, forgiveness and the "Amazing Grace" of God.

Reverend Bob Kraning
March, 2006
Originally appeared in *Trading My Sorrows*

Prologue

There I was, 30,000 feet above the earth one hot mid-summer day in 1981. In a short time, I'd arrive at the Denver airport, and then endure an additional five hours traveling in an old Greyhound bus until reaching my final destination, Trinidad, Colorado.

Trinidad was an old mining town tucked away in the southeast corner of Colorado. Much of the town's vitality had faded with the decline of mining until the early 1970s when the town became center stage for an entirely different reason: the treatment of gender dysphoria. One surgeon and one hospital together specialized in performing a radical surgical procedure thought to be effective in treating gender dysphoria, a disorder of identity. People needing treatment flocked to Trinidad from around the country.

Dr. Stanley Biber, a former Army M.A.S.H. surgeon, had performed almost 3,000 of the treatment surgeries at Mount San Rafael Hospital since 1969. The hallways of the 70-bed facility bustled with nurses and doctors, and curiously, also nuns, who cared for and comforted patients before and after surgery. The shopkeepers and restaurant owners in town were accustomed to the unusual clientele. "It's a boon to business here," Dr. Biber was later quoted as saying in a 1998 New York Times article. "They come with families, they stay in the hotels, they eat in the restaurants, and they buy at the florists."

I had been approved for the surgical treatment by Paul Walker, Ph.D., the nation's most renowned psychotherapist for gender dysphoria, and co-founder of the organization which wrote the guidelines for evaluating and approving potential candidates for surgery. As the saying goes, "He wrote the book." The procedure was expected to alleviate my debilitating psychological distress. I had been seeking help for more than 24 years. Now only two days to go and I would finally be at peace.

I arrived and got a room in a small motel late that afternoon. I was exhausted and even a little apprehensive about what I was doing because I was there without the knowledge of my wife or anyone in my family, or in fact, even my very closest of friends. The radical treatment, known in medical circles as vaginoplasty, was more commonly known as gender reassignment surgery. I'll just call it "the surgery."

Gender dysphoria is a deep depression or a disturbing dislike of one's birth gender. The radical treatment was designed to eliminate the depression by changing the person's outward appearance to that of the opposite gender, and I was aware that nearly 3,000 success stories to date were due to the treatment available in Trinidad at the hands of Dr. Biber. I knew I wanted to become another person. Over the years, that person had taken a name: first Christal, then Andrea, later Laura. Would the surgery truly be the treatment I needed? The surgery would allow me to change my gender from a male to that of a female. I wondered, "Is that possible? Can they really do that?"

The following morning I had my first appointment with Dr. Biber for pre-operative details. Only one more day until the surgery that was the only known treatment to resolve my gender dysphoria. I thought this would stop, once and for all, the conflict that tormented me since childhood. Dr. Biber satisfied himself that I was an appropriate candidate for the surgery when he reviewed Dr. Paul Walker's letter saying so, and when I paid him $7,500 cash for the surgery and agreed to pay the additional hospital fees. It all seemed so incredibly easy.

Dr. Biber instructed me to go from his office, located in the old bank building, take a cab and go to the hospital for the pre-surgery blood work, and complete the financial payments for all the hospital costs.

I remember feeling like I was in dream that I couldn't wake up from, a dream that I had no power to stop, although I wanted to. Walking into the hospital after the cab ride, I started getting a very sick feeling. I was sinking under the weight of the secrets, the lies and the overwhelming pain of nearly forty years of struggling with the nearly constant chatter from the girl who lived in my head. She was with me from a young age, and I couldn't get her out of my head, not even for one day. At this moment, in this hospital, in this waiting room, I had never felt more alone, more twisted or more powerless. The overall effect was like I was watching a dream, and that I had as little control over events as the one who is sleeping. The only thing I could do was watch in dismay.

Suddenly, though, I snapped awake, it was no dream, it was about to be a horrible nightmare. I found myself in control of my feet, and I got them moving: Get up; get out! I started walking aimlessly through the streets of Trinidad. Why, why, why does amputation and mutilation seem like the only way to resolve this ongoing and tormenting conflict I had endured all my life? Was surgery really the way to resolve the conflict? I was walking and weeping up one street, down another. "What was I doing?" I thought. I had given so much thought to this, it must be the way, but I wanted also to be the husband, father and man God had created me to be. How could the girl in my head hold such an overwhelming powerful grip on my thoughts, behaviors and identity? I remembered who God was and how powerful He was and how wonderful my children were. I have the best kids and wife in the world—how could I do this to them? How could I do this to myself and my body?

I walked for over an hour, arrived back at Dr. Biber's office in the old bank building and advised him I was not going through with the scheduled surgery the following morning. He calmly said "Okay, if you want to come back at a later date, I would be happy to perform the surgery when you are ready." Dr. Biber refunded one-half of his fee, and I was happy to have escaped with my body intact.

Now I was back on the bus, riding five hours to the Denver airport where I would grab a flight back to Los Angeles. I would go home knowing it was time to confess to my wife what I had almost done in that little town in Colorado. I was sure that the Lord Jesus had helped me escape having the surgery, but I knew that my wife would not be pleased I had lied to her and kept a secret that would have such a devastating impact on her. I had lied to her plenty of times before. I knew the gravity of what I would face during my confession.

When I came home to my wife and family that summer of 1981 and privately confessed to my wife what the real purpose of my trip was—radical surgery—it was not me who went headlong into pain, it was not me who could not stop crying, it was my wife. She was in more pain at that moment than I had ever been in.

Her pain gave way to anger and I deeply sensed the awful hurt and betrayal with which she was now dealing. I knew from her response that the marital relationship that had struggled at times was coming to an end. My alcoholism and constant gender twisting were barely tolerable, but this surgery was the end. Even though I told her I would overcome this lifelong desire, she was finished with me. I hated who I had become.

I did not want to end the marriage, I wanted to try again to become the husband, father and man God had created me to be. But as much as she wanted to, my wife could not continue in the 19-year marriage. I did not blame her—well, that's not true—I was blaming everyone: my childhood, my alcoholism, the pressure of my job. I could not find it in my sick little head to accept responsibility for anything. At that time I may have wanted to claim I was kidnapped by mental aliens, taken to Trinidad, Colorado, and forced at gunpoint to have the radical treatment. My daughter was 16 and my son 12 at the time of the separation in 1981 and final divorce in 1982. This was the first of many low points in my life.

I was in the thick of a battle that I was not able to adequately explain or understand, a battle between the male gender into which I was born—Walt—and the female gender of the tormentor that lived inside me—the girl known as Christal West. Christal's existence had begun innocently enough at my grandma's house—grandma's house, thought to be a safe place, but we had to hide what we were doing. Over time, Christal was no longer satisfied with being stuffed away inside the body of a man, and she nagged me about having a life of her own.

Christal's first triumph was when she convinced me to undergo female hormone treatment with an "underground" doctor in Beverly Hills in the mid-1970s. Taking female hormones seemed to give Christal an edge, some extra power over me. She started using a new name, Andrea West. Her next maneuver was getting the tummy tuck, a botched surgery to remove sagging skin from excessive weight loss, but whose resulting infection nearly killed me. I stopped the hormone treatment, but Andrea remained.

My mind would often just drift away to this fantasy-land that had no pain, a retreat which even though short-lived, was a welcome place to go. But I knew better than to tell others about Andrea's existence, and hiding became a source of shame, which hurt me all the more.

How did she get inside me? How could she have so much control and power to destroy me? Well, travel with me and come to your own conclusions.

Chapter 1.

Growing Pains

For the last twenty or so years, it has been popular to evoke the excuse "I was raised in a dysfunctional family" as the cause for everything that goes wrong in a person's life. My view is that the first step in being able to make positive changes in life is to take responsibility for our behaviors and not to blame others. I didn't always think that way, and I wasted time in the "blame game." That said, I also believe that to know myself as an adult, I need to know who I was as a child and what happened to me during my formative years. To help you understand how I got to that hospital in Trinidad, Colorado, I need to share some of my early life with you.

My parents no doubt loved both my brother and myself very much. My brother was very different from me. He rarely got into trouble, was not a running, jumping or an active child as I remember—more of a bookworm. He studied, was not quick or impulsive like me.

I do not blame my parents for anything. They did the best they knew how, and with me in particular as I know I was not easy to raise. I was extremely active and a bit mischievous, and I was guided more by my rules than by my parents' requests to slow down and read a book like my older brother. I was just different.

It wasn't all bad when I was very young. All the neighborhood kids came to play in the vacant field next door. As I remember, my mom would put my brother and me in the bathtub and scrub us down, removing the evidence of a day of playing in the dirt field. Mom dried us off, dressed us in our pajamas, and lovingly tucked us into bed. Kneeling or sitting at our bedside Mom would pray with us, "Now I lay me down to sleep. If I should die before I wake, I pray the Lord my soul to take. Amen."

Because it was war time, military planes could be seen in the skies by day and their engine noise heard at night. I had no perspective of how far away the battle was. I remember being scared that a bomb might blow up our house, like the pictures I saw on the front page of the Los Angeles Times newspaper. Is that why Mom was praying: "If I should die before I wake"? I started waiting longer and longer to go to sleep. My older brother, on the other hand, would fall asleep almost as quickly as Mom turned out the lights and exited the bedroom we shared. I would lay there wondering if I would die when I fell asleep. The frequent noise of the aircraft above was unsettling to me. During the day I watched them fly by and tried to tell which planes were fighters and which were bombers. My dad would bring home great color pictures so I could learn about the different military planes used in war.

My dad's mom and dad lived within three or four houses of us, and frequent visits on weekends and weekdays were part of the family dynamic. Grandpa was a little guy that would never say a bad word, was always very busy and polite. My grandma was a little bossy, very demanding, but when she wanted, she could be charming. The charm was mostly reserved for non-family members.

My father held two jobs during the war. By day, he was a salesman for a small belting and rubber company; by night, he was an auxiliary Los Angeles police officer filling in for the regular police force who had been called off to war. My grandfather, Dad's father, also filled in as an auxiliary detective assistant in the same police division.

My father was a rigid disciplinarian and yet I was prone to hang close to him. My father loved his boys, very proud. I remember him working in the backyard which was a steep hill, digging the dirt to carve a level place for my brother and me to play. I tried to dig with his big shovel, but the handle was too long and the shovel a bit too heavy.

The very next day when my dad arrived home, held tightly in his grasp was a shiny kid-sized shovel with a bright red handle. Wow, my eyes sparkled at the sight of it. My dad said "Here, this is yours. Let's go try it out." He carried that shovel to the dirt area where the previous day I had attempted to dig, but now with that little red-handled shovel in hand I was able to penetrate the earth and begin to dig bit by bit. It was here I learned the joy of working to change that dirt slope, unusable as it was, into a flat area where my brother and I could play.

My dad planted grass, grass that my mom would regret he had ever planted. Grass stains appeared on every pair of pants, every shirt, even my socks. It was evident where we spent most of our days playing. Both the nightly prayers by my mom and the red-handled shovel given me by my dad were loving presentations by my parents. I didn't doubt that they loved me.

My parents believed in disciplining me. When I did something wrong, and that seemed to be all the time, I received a whooping. I vividly remember the spankings when I was maybe three or four years of age. My mom would very briskly grab my arm, jerk it skyward with such force that my little feet swung in mid-air. Then with her other hand, she struck my back, my butt, wherever she could land some smashing blows with her open hand, counting one, two, three, four, five. I would be screaming at the top of my lungs, kicking my legs, yelling, "Stop! Stop! Stop!" I was so small that she could inflict a good measure of pain with this regimen. The problem was that I angered her frequently and she delivered her discipline with ever-increasing force over the years.

I loved my dad. But he would tell me to do something and in the manner of kids everywhere, I'd asked, "Why?" Or I'd move too slowly, and he said I talked back. That may have been true but his discipline was even more severe than my mom's. He would have me drop my pants, bend over, and the hardwood floor plank reserved for spanking was pressed into service across my tender buttocks, delivering crushing blow after blow. My little knees would buckle. He would grab me and pull me up while I was screaming at the top of my lungs with pain, and continue the delivery of discipline. I remember the days after these spankings standing on the toilet seat straining sideways to look into the mirror that hung over the bathroom sink to see the bruises I had sustained.

But there came a time when the discipline no longer brought me physical pain. In fact, I delighted in not crying during the frequent spankings. But the pain of the spankings was stored up inside me and one morning I awoke crying. I hadn't been spanked that morning, but I was crying as if I had been. My mom tried lovingly to console me, but that day I could not stop crying no matter how hard I tried. My mom became increasingly angry at my persistent crying and started telling me to stop acting like a baby. "I will put you back in diapers if you're going to act like a baby." But I was in pain I was not familiar with, and the crying continued throughout the day. My mom became more and more distant and resorted to name calling: "You're just a baby" and "Stop acting like a baby." But I was in pain. When my father got home in the afternoon I was laying in bed, the crying reduced to a whimper. He talked to me gently at first and my whimpering turned to crying. He told me we were going out to dinner as a family, but if I did not stop crying I would stay home alone. That comment only served to ramp up my crying which made him angry. So my mom, dad and brother went off to dinner without me. I was under ten years of age.

I stayed home in bed and cried myself to sleep. The next day I seemed okay. That following weekend my parents went away and as usual, my brother and I went down the street to stay at my dad's parents' house. My sleeping place was the couch in the living room. After the lights were out, I needed to go to the bathroom. But I could not get awake and off the couch quick enough. My bladder emptied and I wet the couch. Scared half out of my wits, I lay in it awake, fearing the discipline I would face.

Well, I was not disciplined by spanking. Instead, my grandma declared I would never stay over at her home again.

My parents were not happy, but no whippings were delivered. But the next time my parents went away for a weekend, my dad made the drive across town to drop me off with my mother's parents, while my brother stayed with my dad's parents (he was a good boy). Do you sense a little resentment?

Anyway there I was with my mother's mother, Grandma Rotramel. Her nickname was "Mamy." She was short, a bit fat, and always wearing an apron with a pocket that held a half-pint of whisky for "cooking." Perched on her lips was a cigarette with a world-record amount of burnt ash dangling intact, hanging on for dear life. Yes, Grandma Mamy cut quite a figure.

Grandpa John did, too. Grandpa John had a wooden leg to replace the one lost when he fell under a train in his early 20s. The leg was severed just below the knee. John was gruff and difficult to everyone except to me—he really liked me. But it was my Grandma Mamy who perhaps started a ball rolling that became the most destructive force in my life, the purple dress. As part of our playtime together, Grandma would help me play dress-up in her clothes. She was a great seamstress and she embarked on making me (a very young boy under ten years of age, I'm not sure of my exact age) a purple chiffon full-length evening dress. I do not know if I requested it or if she just did it all on her own. I stood on a footstool as she fashioned that dress, piece by piece, just for me. I liked what she was doing. To keep it a secret, the dress remained at her house, to be used when I stayed over without my brother for the weekends. It became a regular part of my playtime to dress up in the purple chiffon evening dress in Grandma's walk-in closet, with Grandma helping me. Grandpa wasn't there on weekends because he drove a tow truck for a Chevrolet dealership, working the clutch pedal with his wooden leg.

The time came however, when the dress did go home with me, because I was enjoying the dress-up and wanted to show my mom and dad my new dress. When I took that purple chiffon dress out of the paper bag to show my dad and told him that I had been playing dress-up at Grandma's, nothing would ever be the same between the two of us again.

Dad exploded, not at me, but at my mom for having a mother who would make me a dress. A major screaming fight broke out between Mom and Dad over that dress. My dad threw it in the trash and emphatically reported that he was not having any sissy for a son. He would make sure of that. The worst of it was the reaction of my father's parents and his adopted brother, my Uncle Fred. My father's parents became standoffish, and Uncle Fred made fun of me because I had worn the dress, shaming me. Without any malice intended on her part, Grandma Mamy with her gift of a purple dress unwittingly set the table not only for my next painful and disturbing experience, but for a lifelong struggle with my identity as a man.

Only in his early teens, Uncle Fred was a little crazy by any standard and he snuck alcohol during the many family get-togethers. Uncle Fred delighted in making fun of me having a purple chiffon evening dress. He focused on my private parts: pulling my pants down, grabbing me there, and calling me a sissy. This was repeated time and again over the course of a couple of years.

Then Uncle Fred got his driver's license. One day he drove me up in the hills above our house to an isolated dirt road where he pulled my pants down, took off the rest of my clothes and grabbed me where he shouldn't have. I cried and ran naked from the old Ford, running for shelter one street below, hiding in the bushes. He slowly drove by and threw my clothes to the ground near me. I grabbed the clothes, dressed quickly and ran home telling my mother what Uncle Fred had done. She said I was lying—Fred would never do that. She told me I should stop lying and she wanted to hear nothing more about it.

When my dad got home, my mom told him what I had reported so that since he was a policeman, he would clear this up. He went over to see his brother and ask him what happened. Uncle Fred said I was lying and that none of what I had said had happened. That's the way it would remain with my family—that I was making it all up. At least with all the commotion directed his way, Uncle Fred stopped making fun of me and stopped grabbing my private parts.

A couple of years later, Uncle Fred joined the Marines and went off to Korea to fight in the war. In Korea, he was involved in some of the bloodiest battles of the war. He returned to the states, fired up to be a great success selling life insurance. He was always a big drinker, but divorce from his first wife, the mysterious death of his second wife, and the fatal car accident sustained by the third wife, really drove him to the brink. He went into a downward spiral of alcoholism, unemployment and poverty, finally living in his camper shell on his pickup truck. For thirty years, Uncle Fred had no permanent address and I had very little contact with him.

When Uncle Fred was around sixty years old, I heard that he was married for a fourth time and it appeared like his life was in recovery. I contacted him and we arranged a time and a place to meet. I was planning to confront him about what I had experienced at his hands some forty years earlier. But three days before our scheduled meeting, Uncle Fred died of a massive heart attack. I only hope and pray it was not his anxiety about our meeting that caused it. I would never benefit from talking with him about what he had done to me as a young child.

As I look back on the milestones from my earliest years through the time I turned ten—the love, discipline, dress-up, molestation—I can see I was happy on the outside, appearing smiling, but inside I continued crying. In my childlike way, I needed to overcome my frustrations and channel my energy into something that gave me joy and fun, preferably something that also would gain the approval of my father and mother, something that was mine and no one else had.

Me as a cowboy

Chapter 2.

A Cowboy's Dream Lost

In the late 1940s and early 1950s, television was the new technology. My dad was the first of anyone we knew to get a TV set, a 7-inch Hoffman, about the size of a small suitcase. The 7-inch screen was so small that an after-market product to enhance it became popular: a giant glass bubble mounted on two metal slides fastened to the TV, so that the glass bubble magnified the picture. Unfortunately, it also distorted the picture.

There were only one or two stations that had programming and even those didn't broadcast all the time. The program I liked most was the Spade Cooley show, a country-western show with Speedy West, the electric steel guitar player, sitting just off center stage in front. I fell in love with the sound of the electric steel guitar and Speedy West was my hero. The guitar music was fast and it made my feet want to tap-tap-tap with the music beat.

I talked up Speedy West so much that some of my relatives, my dad's older sister, Betty, and her husband, Cliff, got involved. Uncle Cliff was a very funny guy who sold Olympic paint to hardware stores all around the Los Angeles area. He knew where Speedy West gave guitar lessons—on the second floor over a hardware store in Pasadena, California. My eyes lit up and I begged my parents to let me have guitar lessons. My mom's friend had a daughter who also wanted guitar lessons, so it was done. Little Peggy and I were now taking electric steel guitar lessons from my television hero, Speedy West, in an old cramped studio above a hardware store in Pasadena.

I thoroughly enjoyed learning how to play the guitar. Both Peggy and I caught on quickly and I loved the sound of the electric steel guitar. After about a year, I had become so good playing "The Electrical Steel Guitar Rag" (a fast moving, very fun song) that Speedy scheduled a Sunday morning radio show where he and I would play it together, on the air. This was extremely exciting for a kid about 10 or 11 years of age.

I wanted a cowboy outfit. Even though it was a radio show, I wanted to look the part of a country-western performer like I had seen on the 7-inch TV screen with the glass bubble. On Friday, my mom took me shopping and I got the best-looking western outfit I had ever seen: a flashy light gray shirt with green silk piping, a white hat, and my little cowboy boots. When I modeled the new outfit for Dad when he came home from work, he clearly was not pleased. Was it the money Mom spent? Was it the way I looked? What was troubling Dad?

Dad wanted to go out to dinner, but first he wanted me to change out of that "silly-looking cowboy outfit." But Mom stuck up for me and I went to dinner in the new duds I would wear on the Sunday radio show. At dinner, Dad had one martini, two martinis, looking at me with some disgust because I had not changed into regular clothes for dinner. He said I looked ridiculous and he was embarrassed to be sitting with me because people were looking. I was devastated, totally devastated. Tears welled up in my eyes but I held back crying. I would not give Dad the satisfaction of knowing he hurt me.

I didn't play on the radio show with Speedy West that Sunday or at any other time. Both Mom and Dad tried to persuade me to go back to taking lessons but I was done. It was too painful. That girl in the purple dress in my head was much safer than the boy in the western outfit with the white hat and cowboy boots playing the electric steel guitar. The girl was a secret that my dad could not ridicule or shame. She became my hiding place.

For a time, I withdrew into my own silent world, safe from the painful conflicts and discipline dispensed by my mother and father, where I spent my time imagining what it would be like to be a girl.

Chapter 3.

From a Youth to a Teen

The next few years of life provided some rest from the external conflicts I encountered as a child with my mom, dad and Uncle Fred. The discipline had vanished. Uncle Fred kept his distance and the 1950s were a very different time. TV sets, stereo systems and new cars reflected a prosperity that was more fun than the war years of the 1940s.

The conflicts I faced now were all internal. The girl with the purple chiffon evening dress had become like a bad neighbor who would not stop making noise and interrupting every good train of thought. That girl in the purple chiffon dress was growing up with me, demanding more and more of my time. She was always disruptive, and I wanted her to take her purple dress and move out of my life, but inexplicably she became stronger and stronger. Although I was only a child, I had taken to crossdressing in Grandma's clothes, my mom's clothes, even sifting through neighborhood trash in search of discarded clothing to use to cross-dress.

Always hiding, I became great at covering it all up. No one ever confronted me about my cross-dressing, so I knew I had successfully kept my secret. But indulging cross-dressing is like feeding a small fire—it just gets bigger and bigger. This fire was out of control. Inside I was divided. I desperately wanted that growing female to go away, but I enjoyed being a female so much that I desperately wanted to keep her alive. At the same time I wanted to be completely Walt. I felt like I was being torn in half.

My brother was always quiet, yet smart. He could build radios from parts, and he loved to read every book he could. I, on the other hand, was a bit of a screw-up where reading and school were concerned. After a short time in public school, my parents attempted to place me in a military school. During the pre-registration interview, I fled outside and declared I would never go to a military school. To my parents' credit, they backed off from the idea.

Back in public school I had lots of friends. Most of them were the best students in my class and were all good kids. I was not good at homework and I earned less-than-stellar grades as a result. I could not concentrate on reading or studying because that girl with the purple dress kept interrupting my thoughts, disturbing my study time, demanding that I give her my time fantasizing about eliminating Walt. The battle went on like this, all day, every day.

I played football and ran track in high school. Although I was too small for varsity football, I had a great leg for kicking the ball and qualified as first-string kicker on the "B" team. In track I was very competitive in the 660-yard run, with a top-ten best time in the city in my senior year. At one of the track finals, I came close to qualifying to compete in the state finals. The five top finishers qualified for the state finals. I finished sixth, a strong showing nonetheless.

I was popular, well-liked, a member of a school car club. I already had a strong work ethic I think came from that red-handled shovel. Starting at the age of twelve I was always working during my spare time: mowing lawns and delivering the newspaper, with responsibility for both morning and afternoon routes. I was earning more than sixty dollars a month, which I stuffed into socks in my dresser drawer.

By the time I was fourteen, I was a car junkie. I bought my first car, a 1941 Ford that had been underwater and was for sale for $15.00. It did not run but my dad was very supportive in helping me set up the garage to bring this old Ford to life. With a rented engine hoist, I pulled the engine out. Now the engine was easy to work on, and with every moment I could spare, I worked to rebuild it, clean it up, and spray-paint it a bright red. I put the rebuilt engine back in the car and got it to run. Now I just needed to add some "flash" to the car. I had the money to buy a throaty-sounding dual exhaust and a bright red $19.95 Earl Sheib paint job for the entire car, to match the motor.

My brother was sixteen, two years older than me, and old enough to drive, so he started using the '41 Ford. He promptly got a ticket for the very loud dual exhaust. Soon after the water pump broke, causing the fan to come off and tear up the radiator. With my car out of commission, my brother bought his own '47 Ford. My family moved to a new house and my '41 Ford sat next to the house, abandoned, until I could fix it. I was still too young to legally drive it.

At the time Christine Jorgensen made headlines across the world declaring she had undergone successful sex change surgery from a man to a woman. In approximately 1955, I came to learn of the existence of surgery that reported to change a man into a woman. Christine Jorgensen was the proof. That was like lighting a match to gasoline inside of me. I wanted to do that. Knowing the change from a man to a woman was possible gave me new hope. I could fantasize about a new life, free from the past. This fantasizing, over time, became an obsession that occupied a major portion of my thought life. No matter how hard I tried I could not drive away the obsession to become a female.

When we moved to the new house, my dad went out of his way to make the new two-car garage into a place where I could work on my old Ford. He purchased some round steel pipes, had someone cut holes in the concrete garage floor to allow the pipes to stand as posts, and fashioned an engine hoist with a cross-bar and chain. Now I didn't need to rent a hoist, I had my own. With the hoist, I could pull the car's engine out of the car, making it easier to work on or rebuild.

I again set out to fix the engine from the '41 Ford in my new garage workspace. But my constant companion in my head was the girl in the purple dress and the thoughts of having surgery like Christine Jorgensen. How long would I need to wait? Or would the thoughts eventually go away? I was not homosexual; I just wanted to know what it was like to be a girl, living a life free from the painful memories that plagued Walt.

My girlfriend Joy and I had gone steady for a year when I finally had the trust and courage to tell her about the girl in the purple dress. When I shared with her the thoughts I was having about becoming a girl, she was puzzled by why a heterosexual man would want to be a woman. She was the first person I ever told about my secret thoughts and my secret cross-dressing. Although the relationship broke up, she never told anyone; she kept my secret. Joy was a person who knew and trusted God. She was a person of faith, more so than anyone I knew at the time.

I got the old '41 Ford running again, but I still wasn't old enough to drive it. I was working hard: making money working at Bob Hartig Automotive, helping a neighbor dig out his backyard, and delivering newspapers for the Daily News every day on my bike. My pile of cash in the sock drawer grew. I sold the old Ford and purchased a 1950 Oldsmobile four-door V-8. Finally I had my license. The Olds was fast, but not fast enough for me. I sold it and purchased a 1934 Ford coupe with an Oldsmobile V8 engine. The coupe cost $1,000, a small fortune at the time, and much to my parents' surprise, I had the money squirreled away in my sock drawer. This '34 Ford had a special paint job—thirty-four coats of lacquer that produced a deep color that in certain light looked like root beer and in other light, maroon. It was the most beautiful paint job I had ever seen. The interior was done in the time-classic tuck-and-roll Naugahyde in off-white. The extra-wide tires and wheels made this fast little coupe the best-looking car at Eagle Rock High School.

By the time I was in eleventh grade, I had had three years of theater arts classes and had even won a Shakespearian speech festival in the eighth grade. When I heard about an upcoming state competition, I tried out at my school to be a participant in the three-day contest at the main stage of the Pasadena Playhouse.

Our drama teacher selected the play, "The All-American Ape" and chose me to play the major role of a little kid named

Harvey. Harvey lived in a high-rise apartment building, and he idolized the All-American football player who also lived there. The play built to a climax. The All-American had jumped to his death. For the last four to five minutes before the final curtain close, I alone held the stage. Removing his All-American trophy football from its stand on the fireplace mantle, I gripped it tightly as I wordlessly portrayed the emotion of losing the idol I loved so much.

It was my best performance ever and I was awarded a screen test by Paramount Studios, who had scouts in the audience for the three-day competition. I was the only one from our school to be offered a screen test. But my mom was particularly biting in her criticism of Hollywood and was vehemently opposed to me being recruited as an actor. Disheartened, I never showed up for my scheduled screen test at Paramount Studios. What I desperately wanted was affirmation from my parents for what I excelled in, and to find my own niche where I could express myself, develop my talents and do something I enjoyed.

During my senior year, I kept very busy running track, performing in plays with the theater club, and hanging out with my buddies in the car club. Outside the classroom, I worked at my jobs, worked on my car, and dated. But the interference of thoughts from the girl in the purple dress kept ringing in my head and nothing I could do would make them go away.

I graduated from high school in summer of 1958; coincidentally, from the same school my dad attended twenty-six years earlier. I took the full-time job as parts delivery driver offered by Bob Hartig Automotive where I had been working for the past three summers. During those lazy evenings of summer, my neighbor, Dennis, and I hung out, going out for hamburgers and thick chocolate shakes, just the perfect treat on a hot summer night.

Dennis was two years older than me and studying psychology at Loyola University. He entertained me with stories about the strange things people do. Somewhere in the many conversations early that summer, I learned that his professor, Father Joseph Caldwell, also did counseling in addition to teaching. Since he taught about how strange people could be, maybe he wouldn't think I was so strange, with my thoughts of becoming a woman. Maybe he could help me make sense of it all.

Without Dennis' knowledge, I got Father Caldwell's phone number and called him to arrange for counseling, and one Saturday morning shortly thereafter, I drove across town to meet with him. He was in his late thirties, kind and gentle. He didn't even charge for his counseling. He suggested that a one-year commitment on my part would be a good start. I didn't tell anyone, not my parents, not Dennis, nobody, that I was now going to counseling, because I would have needed to answer the sure-to-follow question of "why?"

By the end of the summer of '58, I was ready to look for a "real job" beyond the automotive shop. A new high-tech company in Burbank, Librascope, was hiring. They had a government contract to develop the electronic guidance systems for the new Polaris missile system. I boldly applied for the position of draftsman, responsible for drawing the schematics for printed circuit boards. Much to my surprise, I wasn't turned down completely. I was hired as a blueprint deliveryman on the Librascope campus. The position required a secret clearance, which for an eighteen-year-old was no problem to get.

Now that I was making real money, I could afford an apartment away from the scrutiny of my parents. I needed the freedom to go to my Saturday morning counseling appointments without lying about where I was going. Using the excuse of wanting to be closer to work, I rented an apartment in Glendale, and cut my commute time in half.

My first home away from home was right next to the train tracks and across from Jessup Farms. The noisy and frequent clatter of freight and passenger railroad cars making the run from the Los Angeles to San Francisco combined with the pungent eye-watering and breath-taking aromas of chicken droppings and cow manure was redeemed by the price: only $65 a month (about a week's wages for me), furnishings and utilities included. I had my freedom.

The sessions with Father Caldwell provided a safe place for me to talk, but my confusion continued to grow. It's painful to remember how much I liked cross-dressing in the privacy of my apartment, how I collected a number of female outfits and indulged in dressing in them every day. I liked cross-dressing, but at the same time, I was deeply ashamed of my secret habit. After my one-year commitment with Father Caldwell was up, with no sign of making any positive progress in my struggles, and in fact, quite the opposite, the fascination to become a woman was growing stronger, I stopped going to him for counseling.

My career at Librascope was on the move. Every day as I delivered blueprints around the plant, I pestered one of the engineers, Bob Holloway, nicknamed "Hard Tack", about getting a lucrative drafting job in his department. I pestered and pestered him until finally he promised me that I'd get the job if I brought him a completed grade of "A" in drafting from an evening class at

A TRANSGENDER'S FAITH

Pasadena City College. I had never gotten an "A" in anything to this point, but motivated by the $1.90 per hour that the detail draftsman job would pay, I did it. Those were big bucks in 1959 for a nineteen-year-old. Over the next two years, I moved up two levels, from detail to engineering draftsman to design draftsman.

Librascope was great, but all around Southern California the aerospace industry was booming. I kept my ears and eyes open for other opportunities. A new branch of North American Aviation, Autonetics, in Orange County, was advertising their job openings. But my desire to make a move would be put on hold by events outside of my control.

Chapter 4.

A Father Lost, a Wife Gained

It was the early 1960s. "Laugh-In" was the most popular television show, Simon and Garfunkel and the Righteous Brothers were popular on the music scene and TV sets no longer had 7-inch screens. The screens had grown to 24 and 27 inches. TVs were huge, heavy boxes that made the living room more popular than the backyard patio. And the United States was smack in the middle of the space race with the Soviet Union.

While I was working at Librascope, new job opportunities were opening up across southern California as aerospace companies located there and won contracts with NASA. I had my eye on a company leading the development of the Apollo space capsule, a division of North American Aviation, Autonetics. But my aspirations were put on hold with some startling news. My father, who owned and operated his own company, was diagnosed with lung cancer at the age of forty-seven. My older brother was away, so Dad needed me to help him hold his company together while he fought his illness. At the age of twenty, I left Librascope and went to help my dad. This time I would need more than a little shovel.

The C. M. Heyer Company, Inc. (my dad and a secretary) was struggling without the full-time focus of its founder, inventor and only salesman, my dad, Charles. Through long hours at his workshop, Dad had designed an aluminum end-fitting that solved the problem of explosions and fires caused by sparks from the steel end-fitting on cargo nets. Dad pursued and received a patent on the what he called the "Mulox end fitting."

Naive, unskilled and largely unfamiliar with Dad's product line of industrial lifting nets and slings, I was no Charles Heyer. I called on the boat launches and large manufacturing companies who used Dad's innovative products to move their steel, aluminum and concrete pipes. I desperately wanted to be the star to save Dad's company, but it was clear that I was unprepared for the challenge.

I was heartbroken on two levels: at the office, watching helplessly as the company Dad built began to sink without his expertise, and secondly, at my dad's bedside, seeing how much pain he was in and how deep a sorrow he felt. Often fighting back tears, he knew he was dying. He did not want to leave us behind.

Dad's company went bankrupt and closed. I found a great-paying job with Autonetics, forty miles away, an eighty-mile round trip commute each day. Dad was in the hospital and then at home, then in the hospital. When the money ran out, he stayed at home. The cancer had wasted away the bones in his back and he was in horrific pain. Massaging him, administering morphine, turning him, talking to him, Mom and I would alternate all-night shifts to care for Dad. I worked all day at Autonetics, then all night caring for Dad, then back for my shift at Autonetics, thirty-six hours straight before getting a single night's rest. I struggled to stay awake at work. My body was wearing out from skipping every other night of sleep. When I was alone, I would break into tears.

One morning my boss asked to speak to me in his office. "I noticed you're not looking good. You're losing weight and you're always tired. What's going on?" he asked. I completely fell apart and cried inconsolably, as I did that day as a child. I told my boss about how my dad was dying, and how Mom and I were nursing him overnight. He said, "Bring me your timecard." As I handed him my timecard, I thought I was about to be fired. Instead he told me, "Don't worry about coming to work. I will sign you in and out every day. You come back when you can. The paychecks will continue without interruption. Just be with your dad as much as you can."

Dad died on Friday, October 13, 1961. I was two weeks shy of my twenty-first birthday. Losing him left a huge void inside me. During his illness, I began to know how much I loved him and admired him, but more importantly, how much I would miss my dad. I had grown to respect how he made friends and how much everyone loved him. Thank you, Lord, for giving me such a great dad, albeit for too short a time. Even as I write this, I cry as I recall the loss of a great friend, a fun father to me in my teen years. I'm consoled by knowing that he accepted Jesus as his savior during his final days.

My dad had lost his long, difficult battle with lung cancer. The Chesterfield cigarettes, which he smoked at a rate of thirty to forty a day, stained his fingers a rusty brown, the only outward sign of something more sinister happening in his lungs.

In my grief, I tried to be a stand-up guy and strong for my mom, but when I was alone, I was sobbing. I sobbed when I would try to go to sleep. I was sobbing when I was driving alone. If I saw a man and a boy together, the pain seared through my heart and the tears fell again. The hard reality hit me that he was gone and I would never again be able to walk at his side as I did as a young boy or just be with him.

The business and Dad's design patent fell into receivership only weeks before his death. Later, a friend of Dad's showed me an article which said that Dad's company was picked up for $25,000 and the new owner sold the patent for an enormous amount of money.

A few months after my father's death, I was engaged to be married. I had always been very guarded about telling anyone about the feelings and conflicting thoughts that I struggled with every day, but I wanted to tell my future wife. I already had rented the apartment in Glendale, California, that would become our first nesting place. To tell her about my female desires, I invited her to the apartment. But I didn't think that simply telling her would convey the magnitude or the gravity of my daily struggle. I needed to show her. So I had her wait in the living room as I went into the bedroom to cross-dress.

My bride-to-be was not really moved by my appearance in women's clothing, a raised eyebrow at most. I did not know what to expect. I had never showed anyone before, so I had no notion of what she might say or do, but it was a rather ho-hum yawner, with little expression. Perhaps I wanted more, perhaps I needed to talk about it with her, but it was over as quick as it started.

A TRANSGENDER'S FAITH

Little more was said about my cross-dressing or my desire for gender reassignment surgery. It was a subject not talked about.

During our engagement time we attended Saint Barnabas Episcopal Church, the church I had attended for a few years with my mom and brother. The wedding arrangements were being made with the priest to perform the wedding ceremony. Because of my struggles, I arranged a meeting with him one evening alone where I shared my desire to cross-dress and my yearning to undergo gender reassignment surgery. He sat quietly, listening, taking it in, almost too quietly. It was uncomfortable as I spilled my guts out, but it was to an Episcopal father, a leader of the flock, someone safe. I delivered all the seedy details of the cross-dressing, the molestations by Uncle Fred, the discipline by my parents, the dream of becoming a woman.

The priest asked if I was a homosexual. I assured him—absolutely not—I never felt the urge or even considered it a possibility. He suggested another meeting alone in order to counsel further. I felt better at the prospect of knowing I had someone to talk to again about my struggles.

The night I arrived for our second meeting, his office was more dimly lit than before, and prominently placed on the desk near me was a six-pack of half-quart cans of beer and next to the beer, a pint of whiskey. I don't remember if any words were spoken before he popped open the first can of beer and poured it gently into two glasses, some for him and some for me. A brisk twist of the cap and the whiskey bottle was opened.

Now I'm puzzled. Is this pre-marital counseling or a beer bust? The priest was drinking the beer and sipping the whisky, encouraging me to join in. I had a sip or two of beer. But I was growing more and more uncomfortable, especially as he stood from his chair behind his big dark wood desk and walked toward me, dressed in his black robe from shoulders to the floor. He sat in the chair next to me and continued to encourage me to imbibe in the mellowing qualities of the beer and whiskey; I refused.

At that point he repeated his question from our first meeting, this time in a weird and twisted way, "Are you homosexual?" Again I told him no. He got up from his chair, stood two to three feet from me and began to unzip his long black robe from the top. When he had it halfway unzipped, I could see his bare skin and that he had nothing on underneath. Soon the robe was off, he was on the floor naked, the "full Monty," inviting me to come and lay next to him. I jumped up and exclaimed, "You've got me all wrong; I'm not that way," and I fled from his office very disturbed.

The assumption by the Episcopal priest that I must be homosexual was not just an unfortunate mix-up, but an obstacle standing in the pathway of grasping the truth. The truth is: I was dealing with an identity issue. I see now that the cross-dressing was a means of escape from living as the boy who experienced so much pain. The new female identity had never experienced the pain, so dressing as the female identity provided a safe temporary hiding place, like a magician's sleight-of-hand trick. Indulging in cross-dressing covered up the pain for awhile, but after the illusion was over, the suffering resumed.

Homosexuality, on the other hand, includes behavior identified by a sexual act. That sexual action gives a person the "behavior" of a homosexual. Homosexual behavior was not in my desires or thoughts; escaping pain was—the pain which originated in my uncomfortable, twisted and tormented childhood. I secretly cross-dressed to relieve my suffering for awhile. I pinned my hopes on the surgery as the way to make my pain relief permanent.

I would never take the time to sit down with that priest and explain to him how wrong he was. He was disgusting to me, and certainly not a person I felt I could trust. I didn't tell anyone for a long time what happened in the priest's office that night, because, like the times with Uncle Fred, I was sure no one would ever believe me, or take my word over that of a priest.

I don't remember what excuse I used to advise my surprised bride-to-be that our usual priest would not be performing the wedding. Our wedding went forward, but with a different priest from an Episcopal church in South Pasadena. Many years later, I saw the homosexual priest on a Los Angeles TV show advertising his new loving Episcopal church in Hollywood that was a safe place for gay men and women to come and worship. That was no surprise to me, and it gave me the freedom to tell the story of what had happened. Finally I knew people would believe I was telling the truth.

As I said, the wedding went ahead as planned in June, 1962. My head was filled with confusion, not about homosexuality—I was sure I was not homosexual—but with the obsession to cross-dress as a female, even during our honeymoon. The guilt and shame of my private fantasies about living as a female fueled my drinking. Only drinking could reduce the stress of it all: trying to be a husband while hiding the torment and struggle that was active every day of my life.

I had naively thought that getting married would be an antidote to the obsession to cross-dress. It only led to even more feelings of guilt. Don't get me wrong here; I loved my wife as I best understood love at the time, what I could not grasp was what

I could do to make the cross-dressing go away. I would do anything to make that happen. I hated the way the it continuously interfered with building a wonderful relationship with my wife.

But I had no power to stop, even though I was married. For me, drinking to excess and cross-dressing at home were as common as a peanut butter and jelly sandwich. Both my new wife and I were trying to cope with this monster in my head, but it was beyond the expertise of these twenty-year-olds. I was struggling between two equally strong desires: the first, to cross-dress, and the second, to make it go away.

As a husband and a man, I wanted very badly to detach myself from it all, to find a safe place free of conflict. Being married by itself wasn't doing it. Just as I kept digging when I was a young boy with my red-handled shovel to carve a playing field out of a hill, now in my twenties, I kept searching to find a path to restoration, healing and wholeness. I reasoned if marriage alone wasn't the answer, perhaps if I could just pour myself into a career and be successful then the torment and obsession to cross-dress would go away.

When we were first married I was working at North American Aviation as an associate design engineer on the Apollo space mission, preparing NASA specifications for cryogenic electrical connectors. But I wanted to do more, much more. I noticed that my neighbor was coming home with a new car about every three weeks. As I looked over with envy one day at the latest new car in his driveway, I decided to find out his secret. I went to the refrigerator, grabbed two cold beers, and went across the street to get to know this neighbor I envied, but had never met. I knocked on the rickety old screen door, and with an outstretched arm offering a newly opened beer, I introduced myself to the tall guy in the doorway, Ed. In that moment, a new career was born for me, one that would last for many years. The cold beer would come to symbolize both the promising launch and the chilling demise of my career in the car business.

My neighbor Ed worked for American Motors as a factory representative, contacting the car dealers who sold the not-so-popular line of Rambler Americans, Matadors, Gremlins, and the marketing flop, the Pacer. It didn't matter that I didn't care for the current product line, working for a car company could be a career with a rosy future, a new start for me, and a great way to expand my skills and broaden my experience. Besides, I was smitten with the idea of driving a new car every 5,000 miles and having free gasoline.

Ed got me a job as a factory representative, traveling from dealer to dealer, helping with warranty claims and customer complaints about improperly repaired cars. The overnight traveling meant having a motel room for drinking and cross-dressing away from prying eyes. Alone with the fantasy or obsession—I was never sure what was so darn powerful—it consumed me, shamed me and tormented me all at the same time.

I loved the job and the people. Bill, whom I hired to help me with dealer warranty audits, was fantastic and we became good friends. With our wives, we would get together sometimes on weekends for barbecue dinners. In fact, Bill and his wife remain good friends of mine today, some thirty-six years later.

As I had hoped, I was successful in the car business, winning sales contests and earning promotions. But my other hope was not realized. The gnawing, aching and troubling obsession with cross-dressing was not going away.

By this time I was a father to a daughter and a son. I was sure this responsibility would overwhelm my cross-dressing desire. I was happily married to a wonderful woman, with two great fun bundles of joy, a great job, good people with whom I loved working, and yet I was struggling all the more. Maybe church, God and the Lord could take away this horribly twisted, bizarre desires to cross-dress and even to become a woman. I knew it was sick thinking; I just did not know how to make it go away.

We as a family started to attend church together. I was determined to become the husband, father and man God had designed me to be. Through the church, my daughter attended a week-long children's church camp. She came home so excited about her experience; she encouraged us to go to an upcoming family camp there at Forest Home Christian Conference Center in the San Bernardino Mountains.

Forest Home was known for family camp in the summer and special father/son or mother/daughter weekends throughout the year. During a family camp weekend, a speaker, Dr. Dennis Guernsey, captured my attention with his teachings of how a father was to live in a Christ-like way, being a servant to his wife and children. He was a doctor of psychology and a professor at Fuller Seminary in Pasadena, California.

During that week-long family camp, I got up the courage to get some private time with him. Unlike the previous time I shared my problems with a reverend, this time I was sure there would be no undressing. Dr. Guernsey was great. I shared the now life-long struggle that was preventing me from becoming the husband, father, in fact, the man, Christ had designed me to be. Dr. Guernsey encouraged me to also share my struggle with the director of Forest Home Christian Conference Center, Bob

Kraning. Dr. Guernsey assured me that Bob was a very warm and caring man. That began a relationship that continues to this day with Bob and his wife. Forest Home was the place where my son, daughter, wife and I all accepted Jesus Christ as our Lord and Savior.

We were a happy family when I was not drinking. I even liked myself. Sober for a year, running every day, most times I felt like I was on top of the world. I was glad to have my new life. I was truly putting in the effort to make it all work. But at the same time, I was struggling with my walk with Christ because of the ever-troubling girl in the purple dress who now had a name. Her name was Andrea, at least in my head.

My current employer, Renault USA, was about to go out of business and I felt ready to take on a new challenge. An old friend from the now-defunct American Motors called from his new employer, Honda, with the news that they were looking to expand their factory sales team. Now this was November of 1978 and Honda was known only for their motorcycles; cars were still a new venture. Their automobiles had not caught on yet with either the auto dealers or the American public. That didn't matter to me. Staying with Renault was a dead-end, so with my friend's encouragement I called his boss Larry at Honda to explore the possibilities.

In the phone conversation, Larry told me that they had just made someone else an offer for the senior district sales manager position, the position I most likely would want. I asked Larry if I could come over that day anyway and just talk about the career possibilities. He agreed. Only a few hours later there I was, in the employment department of American Honda Motor Company talking with Larry, the zone sales manager. We hit if off like old friends. He said I had just the skills and experience they were looking for in a senior district sales manager, and it was too bad they had already extended the job offer to someone else. Jokingly I said, "Why don't you call the guy you made the offer to and tell him you found someone more qualified, and I'll take that job?" Larry smiled a bit and said, "I can't do that." He asked me to wait a minute.

When Larry came back he handed me an employment application to complete. When I finished twenty minutes or so later, he took my application with him out the door, leaving me to wait. About thirty minutes later, he came back in and said, "I called your references and they all said you are a star. Do you want the job? It's in the San Francisco, Napa Valley and Lake Tahoe areas." I jumped at it. I knew I had sobriety and the Lord on my side. It would be a great fresh start for me and my family. I accepted to start in early December, 1978.

Chapter 5.

Intermingling of Three Worlds

In 1978 "Grease" starring John Travolta and Olivia Newton-John was top at the box office. The premier of "Mork and Mindy" on ABC showcased the talents of a hot new comic, Robin Williams. Kenny Rogers was soaring in popularity due to his hit album, "The Gambler." I had been married sixteen years. My daughter was fourteen; my son was ten. We were a family. I was still struggling, but I felt like I had the wind at my back, my troubles no longer holding me captive. I had a year of sobriety. I was going to become the man the Lord designed me to be.

I started my new job at Honda. The first week was spent in orientation and becoming familiar with the staff and management. American Honda Motor Company was quite small at the time and an easy work environment. As senior district sales manager, I had attained a new level of pay, far beyond anything I had earned to this point. After the week of orientation, I was off to my new sales district in Northern California, to start two weeks of training under Dan Crowe, district manager for a nearby district, the metro San Jose area.

Dan picked me up at the airport and he said he was my chauffeur for the next two weeks. The training period was intense, and I would not have the time to go home to Southern California. There wasn't even any point in having my own car during that period. I was now responsible for all product marketing, facility upgrades, advertising and sales training for the sixteen dealerships in San Francisco, Napa Valley and Lake Tahoe. Dan would personally introduce me to the sixteen dealers to get me started.

Dan was a good guy. He had been with the company less than a year. That night I checked into my hotel in Palo Alto, near Dan's home and we went to dinner together. At dinner he ordered a drink and asked if I wanted one. I declined. Dinner was over and he ordered an after-dinner drink, again asking if I wanted one. Again, I declined. He wanted to introduce his wife to me, so with dinner completed, he drove me to his home where he introduced me to his wife. Dan then opened up a bottle of wine, poured himself and his wife a glass, and one more time asked me if I wanted a drink. I was starting to wear down by the repeated requests to join him. He wanted to know about my drinking habits. I explained that I had stopped after years of too much drinking to excess. He told me that this job required drinking with dealers, that they would think it odd if I did not drink at least a little. The saying was: "Car dealers don't trust people who don't drink."

Now here I was: sober, working on developing my relationship with Jesus Christ and being a good husband and father to my wife and children. I started to rationalize. I needed to be successful at my career, so a drink would not be such a bad thing. And after all, I had the strength of a year of sobriety and Jesus on my side. I thought I was invincible. So I made the choice that night to develop my relationship with Dan, whom I had known only for one day, to get in his favor, to show him I was one of the good old boys, by having a drink right now. What I could not foresee was that my appetite for alcohol was unquenchable. I could not satisfy my thirst for it. I could not get enough. That night I became very intoxicated at Dan's home. Only looking back do I have the perspective that my only concern at the time was with developing a relationship with Dan, and in the process, I turned my back on Jesus Christ, my wife, and my children.

Dan and I developed a good relationship, fostered by our common careers and drinking every night. What was taking place within me was overwhelming shame—shame for my drinking and for hiding it from my wife and kids. That shame empowered the girl in the purple dress—she had always been my escape from shame. After the two weeks were over, I returned home, full of lies about my drinking. I told my wife I was sober. The lies only magnified my sense of shame, the shame that fanned the desire to become a female.

For months, I was gone Monday through Friday working in Northern California, alone at night in motel rooms in unfamiliar places with a very liberal expense account. Every night I found myself sitting in some darkened bar, next to some fireplace, just drinking and staring at the flames, alone, wondering how much I could drink and still drive back to my motel room.

On the Work Front

My job was going well because I was a no-nonsense, no-shortcut kind of guy. I drank hard, but I worked harder. Only a few short months after I started with Honda, along came the gas crisis with its shortages and long lines, and its huge influence on consumer car-buying behavior. Honda's cars became very popular very quickly, along with Toyota's. The big competitors GM, Ford, and Chrysler faded in their popularity due to their cars' gas-guzzling ways.

Wanting to take full advantage of the American consumer's desire for small, fuel efficient cars, Honda challenged the 42 district sales managers representing every key market in the United States to a sales contest. I really went all out for this contest. I was determined to light a fire under my dealers and in the process, become the number one district sales manager in the country.

The contest ran three months. The first month I was lagging behind, maybe in fifteenth place or so. By the second month, I was in third place, my San Jose friend, Dan, was in second. I pushed my dealers to pump up their advertising spending budgets by $10,000 to $30,000 with the promise to reward them with extra allocations of cars if they would step up. Since Honda dealers were demanding and getting one thousand to three thousand dollars over the window sticker for the popular Honda Accord, an extra allocation of Accords was an appealing incentive for dealers to cooperate.

It all paid off. At the end of the three months, I was number one. I had outperformed the other 41 U.S. sales managers and caught the eyes of the national sales manager and the vice president. I was the star in the entire U.S. sales division. I received my gifts for winning the national contest, including a trip to Spain and Tangiers with a select group of Honda dealers, the national sales manager, and others from the upper Honda management.

The popularity and scarcity of Hondas began to breed a level of corruption that I had never experienced before. Within Honda a new culture formed—one of taking bribes in return for arranging franchise opportunities and allocating cars. The staff shamelessly and openly talked about the "G&C" account, which stood for "Graft and Corruption."

Honda wanted to expand its dealer network into new markets and existing Ford, GM, and Chrysler dealers wanted the new action. A Ford dealer approached me with $25,000 in cash in return for my influence in rewarding him with a new Honda franchise. I told the dealer to take a hike. He thought I meant that I wanted more money, but in reality, I wanted no part of it and frankly, at the time I could not help him.

Existing Honda dealers wanted more cars from the scarce Honda inventory. And they would pay "under the table" to get more. This created another opportunity for feathering the G&C account. Every month, cars that were damaged in transit from Japan were sent out to get repaired and when they returned, they were "extra" cars–that is, they were available. The bosses could trade them to dealers for personal favors. With Honda Accords selling for at least $1,000 over window sticker price, just nine cars on a car carrier represented almost $10,000 to a dealer. Dealers were happy to share the spoils with Honda management in order to keep it coming.

One of my dealers placed $2,000 cash in my coat pocket and asked for some extra Honda Accords. I grabbed the money from my pocket and slammed it back on the dinner table, saying "No way!" He began telling me of the other dealers who had been giving their Honda sales representatives "money for cars." I explained that I had not and would not participate. He was angry with me, but I would get his attention on his next allocation of cars. Dealers were not allowed to order the cars they received—it was my job to order cars for each dealer. They got what I gave them, like it or not. That was the Honda way and it gave district sales managers like myself significant control (within guidelines) over their dealers. So because this dealer attempted to bribe me for more cars, I wanted to get his attention to drive home the point. I stung him hard where I knew it would hurt. On his next allocation, I gave him all blue cars, the least popular of the available colors. And I made sure that all his blue cars were equipped with automatic transmissions, the least popular configuration at the time. He was furious. He called Larry, my boss. Larry called me laughing—he thought it was the funniest thing he had ever heard.

Over the course of the next year or so, my hard work and various strategies for advertising and placement of new facilities paid off. My sales region became the fastest growing Honda region in the country, even overtaking Toyota for a short time. But the freedom associated with being a sales representative permitted me to live three distinct lives: successful, hard-drinking businessman, picture-perfect loving father and husband, and twisted transvestite.

On the Home Front

After many months of commuting home on weekends to southern California, I moved my family north to a home I purchased in Sonoma, just north of San Francisco. The five hundred mile move was not a popular one with my wife and fourteen-year-old daughter. I loved my family, but I was so into myself that I didn't really care that they had to leave behind all their friends. My son, on the other hand, was ten and he really liked the adventure of a move.

I tried to do things as a good husband and father. My daughter and I had fun playing tennis together and I took her on "dates" to special dinners at fancy restaurants. My son was absolutely a joy to have at my side, no matter what I was doing. One day we walked past the window of a bicycle shop, and marveled together at the BMX racing bike prominently displayed there. Inspired, with a twinkle in my eye, I approached the sales clerk and with great flourish, I bought it for my son on the spot. His eyes were as big as saucers. It was worth it, to see him so happy. He still has that bike today, twenty-five years later.

In My Twisted Mind

I was now a full-fledged alcoholic, living in complete denial of my problem. Here was the strange part. The excessive drinking at work and the associated shame of hiding it from my family increased my raging desire to become a woman. I began stealing away to the seedy part of San Francisco known as the Tenderloin, frequented by transvestites (cross-dressers who appear in public), male and female homosexuals, drug dealers and prostitutes.

At first, I just drove by, looking at the underbelly of society. Later I got out of my car and frequented the bars, making friends. Cross-dressing in public was the next step. Pretending to be a woman in public could be a dangerous thing to do in certain parts of town, but in the Tenderloin men acting out were commonly seen and tolerated, even accepted. Using a new friend's nearby apartment as a dressing room, I changed into my woman's clothing and applied make-up, while my friend arranged my hair.

For an hour or so, I hung out masquerading as a female in the Tenderloin bars, then cleaned up and headed home for the evening with my family as if nothing had happened. Even though my intentions and desires were not sexual and nothing ever happened that way, by hanging out in such seedy places, dressed in such a get-up, I was clearly turning my back on my wife, my children, and on Jesus Christ. I was too ashamed now to attend church. At the peak of success, I was also at the peak of my desire to undergo gender reassignment surgery.

A "girl" at the Roadrunner Bar who was a transvestite knew how to get on track for the surgery. I went to the doctor she recommended and started taking female hormones. The hormones didn't seem to do much, other than have a slight tranquilizing effect and lower my libido.

Under the premise of a "business trip" to one of my dealerships in Lake Tahoe, I had large breasts implanted by a plastic surgeon known for his work in the transsexual community. After the surgery, my disheartened wife wanted nothing to do with me sexually, which didn't matter to me, since my desire for sex was gone anyway. I was too selfish to care about anything but me and my desire to be female. To hide the breasts under my business suits, I flattened them out by wearing a wide strip of elastic.

After almost two years of excessive drinking, and cross-dressing, I was finding it increasingly difficult to hold my life together, to maintain being a father and being a success at business, while being torn apart inside by the desire for surgery. The three worlds were tearing at each other, with an explosion imminent.

Chapter 6.

The Wheels Start Coming Off

My career could not have been better; my twisted, tormented head could not have been more screwed up. In 1981, just a little over two years after starting with Honda, I was offered an incredible promotion to national manager of port operations, reporting to the vice president of auto distribution. I was very messed up in my head: an alcoholic wanting to have surgery to quiet the turmoil in my mind while getting the biggest promotion of my career.

This would require moving my family back to familiar territory, the southern California area near Grandma and Grandpa. We returned to Newbury Park, about fifty or sixty miles north of Los Angeles. We had lived here in the 1970s during my time with American Motors. We had attended church and made time to go to Forest Home Christian Conference Center for church camps. When we returned here in 1981, the church, the family trips and father-son weekends at Forest Home were all in place.

In my new job, I monitored the ports of entry all across the country, including Puerto Rico and Hawaii. The Honda ships arrived from Japan bulging with cars for the U.S. market. To perform the duties of national port operations manager, I was often on a plane every day of the week, flying to different ports to meet the ships and oversee the discharge of cars off of the ships and onto trains or trucks. There were ports in New Jersey, Virginia, Florida, Texas, a railhead in Naperville (a suburb of Chicago), Oregon, and in northern and southern California. The job was huge, more demanding than anything I had ever done before.

When I had business at the port of Richmond, only minutes from San Francisco, I would hang out again dressed in woman's clothing at the Roadrunner Bar in the Tenderloin district, to experience what it was like to be "out" in public as a female. Using the information I gleaned from the bar patrons and staff, I arranged a meeting with Paul Walker, Ph.D., to lay the groundwork for the surgery. After only two visits, Dr. Walker diagnosed me with gender dysphoria and approved me for surgery. He had seen me on many occasions at the Roadrunner Bar. Imagine! I was married with children, a successful executive with a major automobile manufacturer, and had approval for this radical surgery.

And so it came to be that in 1981 I decided to end the lifetime of waiting and do the one thing I believed would make my mental anguish go away, once and for all. I scheduled the surgery in Trinidad, Colorado, in the skilled hands of Dr. Biber, the renowned (in transsexual circles, that is) surgeon who pioneered the surgical treatment for gender dysphoria.

Depending on whom you talked to, I was going on a "business trip" as I told my family, or taking a "vacation" as I told my employer. Lying came so easily to me now. There's a saying: "How can you tell if an alcoholic is lying? His lips are moving." My true destination was Trinidad, Colorado. My true purpose was surgery. I shared the details with you earlier: how I panicked and walked the streets of town, torn apart by the conflict raging in my head, and finally I backed out, and returned home to tell my wife what I had almost done.

Combined with all my drinking, lies, and broken promises over the years, this secret trip to have surgery was the final blow for our marriage. I wanted to continue to try to overcome the problems that had plagued me nearly forty years, but my wife wanted no more of my "stuff" and within a short time she asked me to move out.

She should have done it years earlier, and to her credit she did everything that was possible to hold the marriage together. She was a good wife and mother. I was at that time, the worst possible husband or father. I had lost touch with Jesus Christ and with reality. I was unfit to be a husband or father. This was the lowest point of my life to date, but I was not finished with my self-destruction. In the coming months I would cause even more shame and despair to myself and my family.

The night we decided to separate, my sixteen-year-old daughter wanted to know if I just stopped loving her mom, and I lied to her and said yes. This lie continues to shame me even today. Facing the truth; why is it so hard? I caused immeasurable hurt in a child because I could not face telling her the truth—that

I was leaving because I wanted to become a female. The lie seemed kinder at the time than telling her the confusing truth.

Somehow the children learned the awful truth of why their mother and I were no longer together. I hadn't told them, but it was obvious that they knew. They did not want to talk about it, and I respected their need to let it alone. Forcing a discussion only would have added to their pain.

Every other weekend, I arrived to take the kids to my place for the weekend. With my children I always dressed as Walt, their dad, to maintain that small degree of normalcy. My sixteen-year-old daughter became so angry at me that she stopped talking to me. If she happened to answer the door when I knocked, she would let me in, but give me the cold shoulder and leave the room without a word. She was so angry that she refused to join her brother for our weekend visits. It would be years before she would let me back into her life, even for a few words on the phone.

My twelve-year-old son allowed me to be a part of his life, but I knew he was finding it hard to adjust to the new reality of his dad being gone, the divorce and the reason behind it. Once, when we were alone eating lunch, he looked at me and said, "I wish you had cancer. At least then I could tell people what was wrong with you." It pained me that at his young age, he felt forced to hide a secret.

It was as if I had exploded a bomb in the middle of my family: breaking their hearts, their dreams, their trust, and shredding any hope of my being the man, father and husband I wished I could be. My troubles were claiming three casualties, all of them innocent bystanders.

My stress level at work was climbing, too. I was alarmed to discover graft and corruption on a large scale at the ports of entry. Investigating some suspicious dealings on my own, I found that one of our biggest trucking contracts was with a trucking company co-owned by a Honda employee and a Honda manager. Both men were profiting from the expanding needs of Honda for trucking.

I also found corruption with the gassing of cars. The way the system was supposed to work was that Honda paid the port contractors five dollars per car to pump two gallons of gas into every car discharged at a port. With a port discharging up to 8,000 cars a month, the contract was worth at least $40,000 per month to the port contractor. But, the graft and corruption version involved an under-the-table agreement between the port contractor and the Honda manager who was responsible for payment. The port contractor did not gas the cars, yet received payment from Honda as if he did, in return for a kickback of cash to the manager. I discovered this scheme because I was getting complaints from dealers that the new cars they were receiving were all running out of gas. I investigated by asking people working in the yard at the port if they were gassing the new cars, and heard that they were instructed by Honda to stop gassing the cars.

When I put it all together, what I discovered was that the manager who was the owner of the trucking company was the same manager getting kickbacks for not gassing cars. The problem was that he was an assistant vice president—and my direct superior. When he discovered I was probing around the trucking company and the port yard asking questions, he became very difficult to work with.

My marriage in shambles, my children in turmoil, and now discovering shocking corruption at the ports under my authority—it felt like the earth was rolling under my feet. I needed an escape and found it in my head, through obsessively thinking about changing my gender.

One Monday morning, my boss, the one with the "creative" income-producing schemes, called me in to our Gardena, California, headquarters. In the privacy of a conference room, he pushed termination papers across the table toward me. I politely told him to shove the termination papers where the sun did not shine and advised him (an assistant vice president!) that he would be the one terminated. I told him I had the trucking company documents listing him as part-owner and the Honda contract with the same trucking company which showed his signature as chief negotiator. The Honda penalty for such a conflict of interest was automatic termination.

When I was done with my boss, I quickly walked across to the other side of the building and walked unannounced into the corporate vice president's office to tell him about the corruption and kickbacks scheme designed and executed by the man who was about to fire me. Within minutes I was asked to take a leave of absence for a time until the accusations could be investigated. Within five days, my boss was escorted off the property and terminated. His trucking company would never haul another Honda. His trucking company had just purchased six or eight new auto carriers to handle the expanding business, but within a short time it would fold due to the cancellation of the Honda contract, its only source of revenue.

As Honda continued its investigation, several other people involved in the scheme lost their jobs. Honda management asked

A TRANSGENDER'S FAITH

me to extend my leave for another month for my own safety, when they verified a rumor that a contract had been issued to end my life. Uncovering corruption at such a high level, which involved unions known for their strong-arm tactics, and believing that my life was in jeopardy, put me under intense pressure.

I was totally alone. Separated from my family, and on leave from Honda, I scheduled counseling visits with the director of Forest Home Christian Conference Center, Bob Kraning. Bob knew of the intense turmoil, anger and pain I was causing my family, particularly my daughter. He heard it first-hand in his separate counseling sessions with my wife and children. He tried to get me to see the reality of what I was doing. But more often than not, I was intoxicated and therefore unreceptive and incapable of listening. The same was true with my sessions with Dr. Dennis Guernsey, the Ph.D. from Fuller Seminary.

I was so mixed up. I took out the breast implants, trying to take away the power that the girl in the purple dress exerted over my mind. She morphed from "Christal" into "Andrea." Funny thing about Andrea, she had different eating habits, different handwriting and a mellower demeanor than Walt. She was a part-time person, appearing in full force when I was home alone. Andrea was hell-bent on having the surgery to become a woman. Walt wanted a normal life as a man.

After Honda finished their investigation, they brought me back in a new position, assistant product planning manager, part of an elite team tasked with the development of a secret product mysteriously called "Project X." Project X became the new Acura division for Honda, a bold move. Honda was the first Japanese automaker to develop and launch a separate luxury brand of cars.

Due to the junkyard in my head, I was incapable of appreciating this fabulous career opportunity.

For the next year and a half, I was drinking so frequently and so much at my favorite bar that the manager honored me with a plaque, mounted over my barstool, declaring that the barstool was reserved for me. At home alone, I drank heavily until I blacked out.

Leading up to this I had had years of therapy. Why was I now a bigger mess than ever before? I had accepted Jesus Christ as my Lord and savior years earlier. Where was He in all this? Why was I not healed by His almighty power? Damn it, this is not how I wanted my life to be. I hated myself for betraying my children. I was beginning to see how selfish and self-centered I had been, but I was in denial that alcohol was my real master, not Jesus Christ.

When the divorce became final in 1982, I had no strength left to battle the female in me. In inexplicable fashion, I gave alcohol and Andrea the keys to my future. A man without the Lord, I turned my back on Him. I gave up on Him because I thought He had given up on me.

But my son, who was devastated by the divorce and even more devastated by my desire to change from male to female, never gave up on me. He more than anyone had X-ray vision and could see the pain in my heart and somehow knew I was not the way I wanted to be. That little guy took the heat from everyone to stand with me in this battle. We hung out, father and son, every other weekend.

Even when I was with my son, the conflict inside me between male and female raged all the more strongly. There I was, motivated by being with my son to be a good father, but torn apart by the equally strong desire to become a woman. Without the benefit of sober thinking, I was no match for Andrea's single-minded pursuit of surgery. I again gained approval from the psychologist Dr. Paul Walker to allow Dr. Biber perform the surgery. This time the surgery was set for April, 1983.

Alcoholics can be baffling and incomprehensible in their way of thinking. I formulated a simple plan for living my life after surgery. I would live as two people, living simultaneous lives. The male, Walt, would continue to work as a male after the surgery, using a male identity. Off-work time would be reserved for the female persona known as Andrea West. This way I thought both the female and the male could each reign supreme, and my conflict would be resolved. This seemed very logical and workable. I thought that I would finally be at peace.

It's hard to describe how the desire for surgery takes over, especially when combined with abuse of alcohol. It took on the appearance of an obsessive-compulsive disorder, like a bulldozer pushing me relentlessly and single-mindedly toward surgery, while destroying every obstacle in its way. Lying, cheating, and manipulating were my tools of the trade. I became expert at persuading everyone that surgery was the treatment I needed. In my compulsion to have surgery, I plowed right through and over everyone and everything that stood in my way. Too bad hindsight always comes too late for us to see how truly stupid our process is.

In preparation for the surgery, I underwent a series of plastic surgeries, such as breast implants, buttocks implants, a nose job, and removal of my facial hair through the painful process of electrolysis. People at work were starting to look at me funny. They knew something was changing with me, but they were mostly silent. If anyone asked, I made up something in my usual cover-up behavior.

I went back to Dr. Guernsey at Fuller Seminary for further psychotherapy in a last-ditch effort to discover how I could avoid this path, but the truth is, my mind was made up and even his valuable counsel fell on deaf ears. I was now beyond asking for help. I was only talking to people who would affirm my decision, which mostly meant my friends in the Tenderloin section of San Francisco. It certainly did not include my family or my employer.

I knew that the wheels were coming off of my life, and it was only a matter of time until the devastating results would be felt. The very thing I so passionately pursued, once it was gained, would devastate me, my family, and my career.

Chapter 7.

The Die is Cast

"Laura, Laura, can you hear me?" It was the surgical nurse trying to wake me up. Walt traveled to Trinidad for surgery; Andrea signed the authorization papers, but told the attendants that a new name would identify the new woman: Laura Jensen. Not Andrea, not Walt, not Christal West, just Laura Jensen.

I had the most wonderful feeling that the weight of the world had been lifted from me. I was in a place of rest deep within me with no battles, no confusion, and no tormenting thoughts. This sense of serenity was unlike anything I had ever experienced before at any other time of my life. I felt good, real good. I was very much at peace, very happy. At forty-two years old, I was finally a woman, or was I?

My boss at Honda granted my request for two to three weeks of medical leave, which I said was for gall bladder surgery. It wasn't a complete lie. I needed gall bladder surgery, so I deliberately scheduled it back-to-back with the other surgery. I figured it made a great cover-up. I had gender reassignment surgery in Colorado on Tuesday, was released from the hospital and flew back home on Friday, then on Monday, drove about a hundred miles to the other hospital for preoperative gall bladder preparations.

My gall bladder surgeon was surprised when I told him about the previous week's surgery. Upon a complete "up-close and personal" inspection, he said that Dr. Biber had performed it well. But he was concerned that my strength would be challenged by having a second surgery so soon. Recuperating from one surgery wasn't easy, from two was certain to be difficult. I convinced him to go through with it.

Well, I came through it, but I was very weak and I hurt all over. I couldn't eat anything solid. When I was released from the hospital a few days later, a friend took me to the home of a lady friend from my Renault days to recuperate for a week at her home at the beach. She thought the surgery was a cool thing. After my week at the beach, I went back to work, following my predetermined plan to be male at work and female outside of work.

I hadn't told my mother anything about any of my femininity-enhancing surgeries. It wasn't just kept secret from her—I had kept it a secret from almost everybody. Mom was retired and living on social security. Her landlord hiked up her rent, and she needed a place to stay until her name bubbled up to the top of the waiting list for a federally-subsidized senior housing project. I thought I could help her out, and help myself in the process. The commute from my condo in Ontario to the office in Gardena took two hours each way, and I would be better off living closer to the office, maybe near the beach. I offered my condo in Ontario to Mom rent-free, and I would rent a place in Manhattan Beach.

Mom liked the idea. The day I helped her move into the condo I broke the news to her about my surgery. Well, as you can guess, she fell apart, crying and talking a lot to make some sense of it. She settled on telling me that she always knew I was different. She kept on telling me how different I had been. Now you might think I would like hearing this, but I had just undergone radical treatment for gender dysphoria. I really did not need anyone, especially my mother, to elaborate on how different I was and apparently how I always had been very different.

Back at work, my product planning position at Honda was turning out to be quite interesting. It was a big change to work at a desk, after so many years as a field sales representative and port operations manager accustomed to being on the road most of the time. I worked closely with outside research groups, such as Chase Econometrics, to develop a profile of the target customer for the new line of cars. It was fascinating work.

But even the thrill of the new job couldn't keep the euphoria of the surgery from wearing off. The confusion started again. This time, I wanted to reverse the radical surgery. My mind was again a battleground of turbulent and conflicting thoughts and desires: aggravating, distressing, depressing, discordant, distorted, unpredictable ruminations that I thought the surgery would have fixed.

No gender change is complete without a change of birth records. My attorney petitioned the court and within a month or two after surgery, the court granted my request. By the order of the California court, my birth certificate was changed: the name Walter James Heyer, male, was removed and replaced with Laura Jensen, female. My attorney advised me that legally I could not continue to work as Walt. Everything needed to be in my new name, Laura Jensen. For months, I resisted. I was uneasy with how my employer would take the news. "They are going to find out anyway," my attorney said. "Better that you tell them yourself, than have it come out some other way."

In mid-October, six months after my surgery, my boss Tom and I met for one of our regular evening meals together. Somehow I managed to get the words out: that I had undergone gender reassignment surgery and my new name was Laura Jensen. As he gasped for air, I thought I may need to call 911 to revive him. He was more than stunned. He asked me to clarify what I had said. I told him again. "I have no idea how to handle this," he said. "I'll need to take this to the president." That seemed reasonable. Having an employee undergo this kind of radical surgery was hardly an everyday occurrence.

About noon the following day, Tom asked me to go home until they could work out the details. I could understand that. They needed to work out the details of how they would handle it with the other employees. Maybe they would move me into an inconspicuous office, away from intense scrutiny.

I kept calling Tom and the answer was always that they "were working on it." Finally, on my birthday, October 25, he said to meet him and the director of personnel at a local restaurant. Birthdays were commonly celebrated, so it seemed possible that we would celebrate my forty-third birthday together.

It wasn't a birthday party. They had their ducks lined up. In return for six months' severance pay, I was to go away quietly. I wasn't ever to tread on Honda property again or discuss my termination with anyone. If I resisted or fought them, they would justify their decision to "lay me off" by saying that my position had been eliminated. They had a document they wanted me to sign. They assured me that fighting the termination would not be in my best interests, and promised that they would make my life miserable if I didn't go quietly. I knew they could make good on their promise. I knew how ruthless they could be. I had seen it. I signed the paper and I was gone.

I was angry. Honda had extensive resources. They could have kept me employed, even if they just put me off in a corner in some quiet department. It wasn't necessary for them to destroy my ability to earn a living. I was obligated to my ex-wife for huge amounts of alimony and child support, negotiated when I had the executive salary, and now I was not able to keep up. Where would I be able to go with my specialized experience, gained during the five years with Honda? It seemed like a waste. If Honda didn't value my contribution enough to keep me on, what hope did I have of finding another corporation that would hire me now, as a transsexual? The realization was starting to dawn on me that my career was over.

Many of my former Honda buddies called to laugh at me. I was the big joke at the office. They felt obligated to tell me the hateful, hurtful stories and jokes being made about me. I was a big joke to all the brass at Honda. My surgery made for entertaining water cooler conversation. But God has a way of humbling people. This was my time—their time would come. Thirteen years later, starting on October 15, 1996, federal juries returned guilty verdicts against many of my mockers, who were sentenced to prison terms for their G&C (Graft & Corruption) shenanigans. They were found guilty of federal racketeering, deeds usually associated with the mob. My surgery was radical and had its destructive consequences, but at least I didn't serve jail time for my mistake.

Over the next few months, interview after interview failed to secure employment. I still needed cosmetic surgeries if I were to pass as female. Since I had lots of time on my hands, and money from my severance pay, I opted for innumerable facial surgeries, skin peels, and hormone therapy. Substantial payments to my ex-wife for alimony and child support drained more of my savings. Without an income coming in, my finances were looking strained, to say the least. To save money, I gave up my apartment at the beach and rented a single room from a guy with a big house.

Completely by accident, it turned out that my landlord was a big-time cocaine dealer. He bought bricks of cocaine from a source on a sailboat, cut it down, and sold it to both upscale and lowlife clients. Cops, store owners, junkies, whoever had money to buy, knocked at the door. The house was hopping with people at all hours, snorting and partying. I had the option to move, but I made the choice to stay.

The thousands of dollars that remained of my severance pay quickly disappeared up my nose as I failed to cope with the pain of a divorce, the continuing torment in my head that the surgery failed to quell, and the complete collapse of my career. Old friends and some family members were now avoiding me like the plague. The evidence that the surgery was a huge mistake was becoming more evident every day. The use of cocaine and alcohol was only adding to my misery, depression, and loneliness.

One night, after drinking heavily, I made my line of cocaine on a glass table, rolled up a dollar bill like a straw and snorted the white dust up my nose. Again and again, I snorted line after line of cocaine. Stumbling around the crowded living room, full of cocaine like some paranoid-schizophrenic, seeing visions of monsters coming after me, I made my way to my room, and came to rest on the edge of the bed. My heart now pounded as if it wanted to come blasting out of my chest. I became rigid, almost like a stone statue. I started thinking I may die. I was totally freaked out and scared. I curled into bed, unable to sleep all night.

The next afternoon I finally pulled myself out of bed. I felt like I was going to die if I stayed in that house one more moment. Still in a drug and alcohol-induced stupor from the night before, I wandered down the street a few blocks to a park to clear my head. I remembered a lady from my days at Renault who had told me if I ever wanted to get sober she knew someone who could help me. I stumbled into a coffee shop near the park and made the call. The following day she picked me up and took me to my first Alcoholics Anonymous (AA) meeting.

I was a disgusting, messed-up sight by any standard: a half-man, half-woman smelling of vomit and body odors after a night spent sleeping outdoors. Beard stubble poked out in patches on my face where electrolysis still needed to be done. Bloodshot and deadened eyes testified to my excessive drinking and drug use. My rabbit fur coat was matted from where I had vomited the day before, lying in the grass at a park in Long Beach. To say I smelled was an understatement. I stunk of the most unpleasant of body odors. I was a mess, both inside and out.

Ashamed, I stayed in the back of the hall in the last row of seats. Everyone else was seated a good thirty feet away, up in front. Even the lady that brought me to the meeting wouldn't sit with me. But she hooked me up with one of the men there, her good friend, Michael. Michael was undaunted by my most repulsive smell and unkempt appearance. I learned later he was actually disgusted but was resolute to help me. Michael agreed to let me sleep in his unconverted garage near the beach during the early phase of my recovery. It was just a garage, not designed for habitation, but Michael's friend Ben agreed to help prepare the garage for temporary living. It was a clean and sober place in which to start my journey to recovery. I had no other option if I was going to live.

My bad choices had destroyed my identity, my family and my career. The surgeon's knife and resulting amputation had not changed me from a man into a woman. I now knew that. The surgery was a complete fraud, a fraud which required a willing participant, me. I realized that it was impossible for any surgeon to completely change anyone's birth gender through surgery.

I had made a horrible mistake by having the surgery, but I couldn't admit it, not yet. So for now I would live life as a surgical woman, an imposter.

— Walt Heyer

Chapter 8.

The Difficult Journey Back

My new friends Michael and Ben were very knowledgeable about the recovery process. They stuck to me like glue, making sure that I went with them to meetings. I didn't have a car, so they drove me there. To start the journey of recovery, the best place for me was in a community of recovering alcoholics and drug addicts who were committed to working the principles of the 12-step program. Ben and Michael held me accountable for working a good program of recovery, meaning rigorous honesty, the very opposite of the lying and denial that defined me as an alcoholic.

During the meetings I found it easy to just open up with whatever I was feeling because it seemed impossible to shock anyone. The stories shared by others at the meetings made my story seem not very different. Laura Jensen, transsexual, fit right in. One example was a husband-wife team. The man was a former Green Beret, a very tall muscular man and his wife was very petite and worked at a horse ranch for most of her life. Shortly after they were married, they both had the surgery. Yes, that's right, the tall muscular former Green Beret and his very petite wife both underwent surgery to change to the opposite gender. So the resulting couple was alarming: the tallest most muscular woman and the smallest most petite man to ever walk the earth. The AA meeting resembled a freak show and I was just one of the many side shows.

I was in a bad way financially. I had no money, no car, and no prospects. I was living off handouts. One of my new AA friends was a caterer, and his clientele included the Hollywood stars. He offered me a weekend job washing dishes and making salads. One weekend I made fifty pounds of pasta salad for a luncheon at Jane Fonda's, assembled with the healthy ingredients she herself specified. During the week, I cleaned houses for AA people who were trying to give me a chance. The former spectacularly successful Honda executive was now a part-time domestic and dishwasher, living in a garage.

Needless to say, I wasn't making my court-ordered child support or alimony payments. My wife was livid. She cut off all visitation rights, allowing phone contact only. My daughter still wasn't speaking to me. My son continued to be my friend. When my wife hauled me into court about the missed payments, the judge ruled against her after he reviewed my non-existent finances. I had no money to give her, so he ended my obligation to pay any support whatsoever.

After a few months of sharing the unconverted garage at Michael's place with his pet turtles, I was offered a much better living situation about an hour away. Ben's mother went into the hospital, leaving her home in Alhambra vacant. Ben asked me if I would go and stay at his mother's to housesit. Well, living in a house was much better than staying in a garage, so I said, "Yes, yes, yes!" What I did not know was that the couple who switched genders, the Green Beret wife and "her" petite husband lived in the same neighborhood. Because we had the surgery in common, and lived so close to each other, we got in the habit of visiting each other frequently. Ben and Michael lived too far away to continue our daily meetings, and I was glad to have some AA friends nearby.

The Lord was at work here for sure. I got a first-hand look at the results of the surgery not only from the mirror where I could lie to myself, but through an up-close (too close) and personal view into the very unattractive life of this "man" and "woman." Within a year after my surgery, in the Lord's own way, he began to demonstrate to me through this couple just how wrong the surgery is. A married man and woman both underwent surgery in the most bizarre "Trading Places" reality episode I had ever seen. It was not appealing.

It was becoming very clear that the surgery they call sex change or gender reassignment is not a sex or gender change at all, but a means to living out a masquerade through the destruction of perfectly good, functioning organs.

About six months into my recovery, the former Green Beret, now a female, came over, all upset at "her" spouse, and asked if I would go for a cup of coffee with "her." As a good recovering AA person, I agreed to go. We got into her car and stopped at a small dingy strip mall not far from the house. But it was not coffee that Jane wanted, it was a bar. Now I was surprised because Jane went to some of the same AA meetings I did and professed "her" sobriety at the meetings. I went with Jane into the bar and watched "her" buy cocaine from the bartender and order a drink. I raised my objections about her actions, but "she" quickly told me to give it up—"she" had been a regular at this bar for weeks. "So where is the rigorous honesty?" I thought.

Being in that bar felt like a living hell: the darkened room, the burning cigarettes leaving a smoky haze that shadowed the people moving about. Bars have their own special smell. The dirty carpet, the smoke and the smell of spilled drinks blended together with an all-too-familiar smell. It was scaring the hell out of me. I felt like I was falling and I was not even drinking. I was in the process of relapse and I had not even taken a drink. I asked Jane to take me home while she could still drive. She agreed, but swore me to secrecy about her drinking. I foolishly agreed.

That visit to the bar with Jane had a profound effect on me. I told my sponsors Ben and Michael about how I went inside the bar and that I quickly went home. I didn't know whether to tell the part about being with Jane or not. I decided she needed to be the one telling others about her relapse, not me. What I didn't consider is the effect that hiding the truth would have on my own program of recovery.

Partial truthfulness is a sign of relapse thinking. About a week later, I was feeling the power of the lure of drugs and alcohol on me. Instead of calling my sponsors, I went on my own to the bar, ordered some cocaine and a drink just as Jane had done the week before. The cocaine, the booze—I was in full-blown relapse.

To this day I cannot or do not want to remember the drinking details of that night. I made my way home safely, but became very, very sick. While vomiting more frequently than I thought was humanly possible, I slowing became aware of the red stain of blood joining the bile in the toilet bowl. I started fainting and became very weak, lying on the floor, unable to stand or even crawl. I was able to grab the phone cord and pull the telephone from its resting place on a table and toward me, and dial 911.

When the firemen arrived they had to break a window to get in, since the door was locked and I was too sick to unlock it. They whisked me off to the emergency room. The doctor wanted me hospitalized. But when the staff discovered that I had no medical insurance or credit card for payment, they refused to provide medical services. So the doctor called a cab to take me home and suggested that I have the cab stop at the store so I could purchase Gatorade, lots of Gatorade, and drink it until I got my strength back. That's all they could do.

When I told Ben and Michael about my relapse, they started spending more time with me so I would not be tempted to relapse again. Beginning my sobriety over, I thought about Dr. Dennis Guernsey. I hadn't seen him since before the surgery, a year and a half ago. His office was only twenty minutes from where I was living in Alhambra. Fortunately, he allowed me to see him. I was in the worst state of mind—more distraught and full of shame than ever, not just because of the relapse, but because it was easy to see that the surgery was destroying my life. I was unable to keep the wheels of recovery on track.

Dr. Guernsey suggested a job with a friend of his that owned a Rocky Mountain Chocolate Factory retail store in Laguna Beach. I agreed, even though it was almost a two hour drive from Alhambra, because I thought having the structure of reporting to work would be good for me. It had been about a year since my abrupt termination from Honda. This would be Laura Jensen's first "real" job, working in a retail chocolate outlet.

With the job in hand, I purchased a cheap car on payments. I tried the job for a few weeks. My job performance was good, but the hours and the drive were too much. Some days I worked from eight in the morning until eight at night, with two hours of driving each way, making it a sixteen-hour day. Worse, I was missing my AA meetings, which could lead to another relapse. So Dr. Guernsey and his friend agreed that it was not the best situation for me at that time and I quit. I asked the dealership to repossess the car, so I wouldn't have to keep making payments.

My mom's turn came for an apartment in federal senior housing, and she moved out of my condo. She had been making the mortgage payments when I could not, but now that was over. I had a good interest rate, the payment was low, but I couldn't afford to pay even that. Now interest rates were at historic highs, and the housing market, especially the market for condominiums, dried up. I asked the bank to repossess the condo, since I knew I was going to default on the mortgage anyhow.

A new Baker's Square restaurant was opening within walking distance from where I was staying in Alhambra, at Ben's mother's house. Ben wanted me to stay in the house if I could. So I interviewed for a hostess position as Laura Jensen. During the interview I lied to cover up my background and the surgery. I said my husband had died and I had no prior employment, but I was sure I could do a great job for them. The manager hired me on the spot.

Once the store opened, I was on hostess duty, dressed in my cute Baker's Square uniform. Having a job with a schedule gave my life much-needed structure. I was like a rock star, drawing a crowd from every AA meeting I had ever attended. They all wanted to see firsthand the transsexual, Laura Jensen, in such public view, performing my duties with great pleasure. Actually it was again like a live side show to real life, me working as a female and not passing as a female with every customer. But I worked as best I could and smiled at my AA onlookers when they came in.

The smile covered up my depression with how my life was turning out. At the two-year mark since surgery, my family life was destroyed, my children devastated, my extended family in disbelief, my career eradicated and now out of reach, and the male man, Walt, torn from the function of life as a man. I was so depressed about the loss of being a father that I was crying myself to sleep. God was showing me how selfish, self-centered and stupid I had been. I missed my twenty-year-old daughter terribly.

Visits with my son, my best friend, weren't as frequent as we would have liked. The Lord knew I needed my son's friendship, as much as he needed his dad. He was devastated but kind enough, or in denial enough, to enjoy our time together. When I visited him, I didn't want him to see me as Laura Jensen. Even with all the terrible events, I was, I am, and I always will be his dad, no matter what. I dressed as a man. Seeing him, even if it was only once or twice a month, was good for me.

I still suffered from very confusing thoughts about my gender: who or what was I? My depression was moving into the contemplation of suicide, even to the extent of planning it, so as to eliminate Laura Jensen and Walt at once. I contacted Dr. Guernsey again, and this time he was alarmed by the depth of my depression and the intensity of my obsession with suicide. He asked me if I would be willing to move into a home with a

Christian family, where they could make me part of their family and of the family of God, in an effort to avoid suicide. I agreed and he made some calls to find a family that would accept a depressed transsexual into their home and family life. He found a pastor who had graduated with him from Dallas Theological Seminary that was open to the challenge. His name was Dr. Roy Thompson, married with two children in high school, with a Ph.D. in cross-cultural psychology and a master's degree in theology. The teens thought it would be fun to see if the Lord could restore such a broken life.

The Thompson family was familiar with facing and coming through tough challenges. When Roy's son Jon was nine, he was struck by a car as he stood innocently at an intersection. As a result, he was paralyzed from the waist-down, bound to a wheelchair. Roy's first wife had caused Roy and the children much pain in her alcoholism. Roy had been married about three years to his second wife, Bonita, an inquisitive, serious career school teacher. Roy's daughter, Kristina, openly expressed her feelings and was very confrontational. Jon, the older brother, was very loving, kind and funny. Roy worked with CityTeam Ministries in San Jose, California, which had a rescue mission and alcohol and drug recovery program for street people and parolees.

At Dr. Guernsey's request, the Thompson family invited me to move to their home in Pleasanton, near San Francisco, and become part of the family. In addition to Roy and Bonita, and the children, Kristina and Jon, the Thompson family had one more member: "Granny," Roy's mother, a very proper high-society Texas woman who loved the Lord. Granny's confrontational nature made Kristina seem withdrawn by comparison. I remember sharing my career experience with Granny one evening trying to impress her. I told her how I had worked on the Apollo space mission project as an associate design engineer, and in the auto industry with Honda, both as national port operations manager and as one of the small team who had secretly developed the new Acura division. I knew that would impress her. When I was finished crowing about my career accomplishments, she responded by saying, "Well, if you're so smart, why did you do something so stupid?" She blew the wind completely out of my sails. I could not speak because I had no answer. The Lord was now using this old lady to get my attention and I was slowly getting the message.

Dr. Guernsey called and talked to his friend Roy from time to time. One time he called because his friend who owned the Rocky Mountain Chocolate Factory store had an opening in his San Francisco Embarcadero Center store. He was calling to offer me a job there, and I was all for it. Unlike the previous situation where I did the driving, the long commute this time was alleviated by being able to use the efficient mass transit system.

I started to work in the summer of 1985. Being a transsexual in San Francisco was exciting. I fit right in. The whole city was a freak show, so I was no stand out. The best part, though, was at the end of the day, when I arrived back at the Pleasanton station, stepped from the bus, and was met by Roy's son, Jon, sitting in his wheelchair, waiting to walk home with me.

The family truly showed me God's love. No matter how broken my life was, they were all going to be there every day for me, just like Jon demonstrated by sitting at the station in his wheelchair with a smile for me. I knew then that I was going to recover. I just did not know how I would ever restore such a broken life, but this loving family was now my family, too.

I opened the door and there before us was a woman in a red sweater fit snugly over her well-endowed figure with bright red lipstick and fingernails and shoulder length hair. "You must be Laura!" I said, inviting her in. Thus began a journey that turned "a few days" into nine months and nine months into twelve more years with visits lasting months at a time.

We had no precedent for this situation in other relationships, nor did we find any specific scripture to act as a road map through this mine field. We did know that we had a responsibility to love her. About this, Scriptures were clear.

- Dr. Roy Thompson

Chapter 9.

Time to Try

It was late 1985, about two years after my termination from Honda, a few months after arriving in the loving arms of the Thompson family, with about a year of sobriety. Now I was realizing I was a man wrapped in a woman's masquerade, a fake, a fraud, a mutilated man. I did not fit anywhere. My manhood had been surgically removed but I was not a woman even though my birth certificate said I was. That was a lie. I didn't want to continue living the masquerade. With the support of a loving family and the help of Jesus Christ, I was truly, with every bit of courage, strength and ability, trying to restore my life to the man named Walt.

It was time to try the strength of my new wings, move out of the Thompson house and get an apartment in town, where I could remain in close contact to my family support system. One little problem existed, though. Walt didn't want to work anywhere that Laura had worked. If Laura originally started the job, then Walt couldn't show up and take it over, and vice versa. It wasn't as simple as changing clothes, telling my employer that I was now Walt, and continuing my employment at the same job. The warring personalities inside of me made sure of that. Now that I wanted to be Walt, I couldn't continue Laura's job at the Rocky Mountain Chocolate Factory store.

Roy helped me find a new job as Walt at a Sunnyvale auto body shop. The owner of the shop was a Christian man with a big heart for helping people who had fallen on hard times, providing they were willing to work. Ed was a very hard-working guy. With his own hands, he had built a very successful high-end auto body repair facility, primarily working on BMW, Mercedes Benz, Jaguar and other high-end automobiles. Ed was a guy with a big heart for helping very broken people. His love for the Lord guided his desire to see my life restored through the Lord's love and grace.

So along with the timing of my move into the apartment in downtown Pleasanton, came a change of employment and persona, living as Walt and working at the auto body shop. Ed and his wife, Kathy, poured out their hearts to help me, knowing it was Jesus Christ who would need to do the work in me, if I did not stand in the way. Ed even invited me to Bible studies once a week with members of his church group. I was not attending AA meetings at all, relying instead on the support of the Thompson's, church and Bible studies.

Initially I adjusted very well to living as Walt for the first time since my surgery. It felt right and comfortable. But over time, my resolve weakened. Living as Walt meant that I felt constant emotional turmoil and pain. I could hardly cope with life. As

Walt, I had been abused as a child. As Walt, I could see the effects of the mutilation I had inflicted on my body through numerous plastic surgeries and procedures, and it didn't fit the appearance of a man.

Life as Laura offered an escape from the pain. The childhood abuse didn't happen to Laura. She lived in relative freedom from the hurts of the past. She laughed more and enjoyed life more. Her female gender matched my body's external appearance. Laura tormented Walt's thoughts, enticing him to switch back. I began feeling more and more fragile, slowly crumbling under the weight of wanting relief from the intense emotional pain, and the pure exhaustion of fighting the intense battle Laura waged inside me to gain control.

I enlisted the guidance of two Christian Ph.D. psychologists to help me cope with my ever-increasing distress. Not wanting to disappoint the Thompson's or Ed, at the end of my rope and not knowing how else to cope, I made the choice to secretly start using a little wine. Well, I was in a full-blown relapse again, just a little over a year from the first one.

Here I was surrounded by loving people whose only interest was my success. What was it that was driving me back to the alcohol and that damn female again that just would not leave me alone? Was this a real life battle between good and evil? How can a little bit of evil take a person from the loving arms of so many who were so kind-hearted? Drinking alone in my apartment is where evil took over.

I was a man who had surgery to become a woman and had had all kinds of cosmetic procedures in an all-out effort to give Laura Jensen a real chance at success. I had a female driver's license and birth certificate, yet I was working as Walt, a male, in an automotive body shop with a boss who was desperately trying to help me. My life was an absurd contradiction.

One day, after drinking all night, I came to work and Ed smelled the alcohol on my breath. The look in his eyes and the expression on his face said it all. Ed was furious, disgusted, and wanted me out of there. He walked me to my car, opened the door, and said, "You're fired." I responded by saying, "Is that the way you deal with difficult issues, just kick them out of your life?" It struck a cord and he relented, "Come back tomorrow, but only if you're sober."

Ed alerted Roy that I had come to work drunk and was now returning home early. Roy was waiting at my apartment when I arrived. I explained to Roy I wanted to be Laura Jensen, that being Walt was just not working for me. This was the beginning of a protracted, pitiful see-saw pattern, back and forth between two genders. Much like an addict uses their addiction to escape temporarily from reality, living as Laura gave me a temporary escape from the pain of my reality. But like the addict, I'd be ashamed of my behavior when the effects of the "drug" wore off. The shame of living a lie propelled me to try living life as Walt again. I'd live as Walt until the pain got to be too much, and Laura's influence too strong. Then I'd switch to Laura, and I'd have some relief from the stress for awhile.

To Roy's credit, when I told him I wanted to be Laura again, he just requested I stay home, not drink, and he would come by to see me in a few hours. In the meantime, Roy found a therapist at the Stanford campus whose career was devoted to working only with transsexuals and transvestites who, like me, were suffering from gender dysphoria disorder, a complete dislike for one's birth gender. Roy arranged for me to start having regular sessions with her. He was sure the therapist could help me control the swings of identity.

The stern and no-nonsense therapist was a member of the Board of the International Gender Dysphoria Association, a group that advocated sex change surgery and living life as a transgender as appropriate treatment for the disorder. She was personal friends with Paul Walker, the Ph.D. who originally approved me for surgery. She took time during the first few sessions to learn my history: my childhood problems, the sense of being trapped in a man's body, and so forth. She said the symptoms and history were typical of gender dysphoria, and that, in fact, I had the worst case of it she had ever seen.

She assured me that the surgery was the proper treatment for my problem. A lot of people who go through the surgery have difficulty at first. My current problems were perhaps attributable to the fact that I hadn't lived as a female prior to surgery. In her opinion, I probably just hadn't given life as Laura enough time.

My boss Ed was clearly disappointed with my alcohol relapse. He allowed me back on the job when I stopped drinking, but I could feel his agitation. His trust in me was completely gone. As Walt, I keenly felt the sting of failure once again.

I knew in my heart that to masquerade as a woman was wrong. I felt the Lord was telling me that I was a man. But the therapist was affirming the surgery and telling me that living life as Laura was the proper treatment for my disorder. Instead of helping me to cope, the therapy was making coping more difficult. The noise in my head grew louder, more deafening. I felt like I was being torn between two genders, yet I didn't belong in either place. I was so uncomfortable in my skin that I didn't want to be Walt or Laura. I had serious issues, with severe pain.

Adding to my pain was how obvious my struggle was to everyone around me. Some nights at home the pain was so intense that I'd stand in the living room bent at the waist with my hands on my knees for support, as I wept and groaned in agony.

I turned to drinking again. One night I dressed up as Laura and went out drunk, confused, and angry. At a bar down the street, I continued my relapse drinking to deaden the storm in my head. Many drinks later I had the answer, a way out. Somehow I hoisted myself up to the roof-top of a local fast food joint, stood on the edge, and began yelling, "I'm going to commit suicide!" The local police came to arrest me for being drunk in public. They put me in the Santa Rita county jail, in a very small cell to sober up. Some hours later I was released, and faced a very long walk back to the burger joint where my car was parked. Thankfully, my car had not been towed away. I drove back to my tiny apartment where the relapse had started, now a broken man and a broken woman. I could not cope with my circumstances. I was truly overwhelmed, due in large part because I turned to alcohol as my savior, rather than Jesus Christ.

When I told Roy what had happened, he was sensitive, but completely out of ideas. He suggested I continue the sessions at Stanford with the transgender specialist. When Ed heard about my episode of drinking and subsequent arrest, he fired me. I was too big a risk. He was right.

At the sentencing hearing for my public drunkenness violation, the judge gave me the following options: go into a recovery treatment facility within three weeks and have the charge expunged from my record, or go to jail for the misdemeanor. The recovery treatment idea was starting to appeal to me.

A TRANSGENDER'S FAITH

I called my transgender therapist to tell her what the judge had offered me and that I was ready to take the recovery treatment option, if I could find one. Well, I showed up for my regular weekly appointment slightly intoxicated. She was mad. "I have no use for a client coming in here drunk. There is nothing that you can say that I want to hear. You will sit there in your chair, in total silence for the full length of your session." Shame-faced, I complied. She completely ignored me as she worked on paperwork.

At the end of the very silent, very uncomfortable forty-five minute period, she slid a paper across her desk at me. On it were with the phone numbers of three recovery treatment facilities in the local area. One of them, the Women's Recovery Association, would hold a bed open for me, but only if I called by 4 p.m. the following day.

Motivated by the judge's ultimatum, I called the recovery house and went for an interview. They showed me the bed that was waiting for me, but first, I was required to go to a 48-hour detox facility starting that very night, or else they would not hold the bed for me.

I went home to my apartment, and called Roy. I was going into a recovery home for at least ninety days and I needed help in vacating the apartment. I disposed of a few things in the trash, prepared a bag of clothes to take with me, and drove over to see Ed and thank him for trying to help me. I apologized for causing him so much difficulty. He was happy that I was going "full bore" for recovery.

With the address of the detox facility in hand, and evening upon me, I drove to a Denny's restaurant near the facility. I went into the Denny's with the full intention of going to the bar in the back of the restaurant and making sure I had something to detox from. Once in the bar, I planted my butt firmly on a bar stool as I had many, many times before in the preceding twenty-four years, usually getting rip-roaringly drunk and as stupid as a wooden stick. Here I was again, wondering: would this be the last time?

I took a couple of sips of my drink, but instead of my going for drunk this time, the weight of shame came over me in a way I had never experienced. So much shame I could not take another sip. Tears slowly welled up in my eyes. It hit me. Everything was gone: my wife, my children, my career, my identity, my self-respect. I was well aware that I was now on the scrapheap of humanity, a thrown-away life, destroyed by my own choices. Alcohol, drugs, and surgery had rendered me useless to anyone. I had failed miserably as the man God had created me to be. In fact, I was a man who was masquerading as a woman, Laura Jensen.

I paid for the drink and drove to the detox facility, an unmarked cinderblock building painted no particular color, with steel doors, bars on the windows and a narrow driveway for parking in the rear. The building resembled a solitary confinement blockade from a horror movie. I parked the car and walked around to the front door. It was locked, so I knocked. A very large African-American woman opened the door. I said I was Laura. She said she was expecting me.

The fee for detox was twenty dollars a day. I paid my two-day fee and cried my heart out as if I were walking to the gallows to be hung. I did not want to be here. This place was full of bums, prostitutes, and court-ordered stays. "Why did I need to be here?" I thought, but I knew it was my ticket into the recovery house. Tomorrow would be my first day sober, May 2, 1986. I had no way of knowing it then, but my life of sobriety was beginning. This time it would stick.

After the 48 hours in detox, I entered the recovery house where I stayed for almost four months. As Laura Jensen, I started again to restore this broken life. For four months, I went to at least one AA meeting per day, often two per day, along with required classes in the recovery home, and daily individual and group therapy sessions. In the women's recovery home, I shared a bedroom and bath with two other women, and all fourteen women ate all three meals a day together. We were never allowed to go from the recovery house alone. Two or more together was a mandatory requirement. I could have visitors, but no one came to visit me except for the transgender therapist. I was grateful to see her. Others, I'm sure, were standing on the sidelines, waiting for the results, perhaps even fearful of another relapse.

This stay in the recovery house brought me closer to God than ever before. The 12-step program talks about a higher power, and I knew it was Jesus Christ. I began to go to church in Foster City, where I met someone who would turn out to be one of the most influential people in my recovery, Pastor Jeff Farrar. Pastor Jeff was a friend of both Roy and Ed. Pastor Jeff allowed me to be very open with my struggle. The Lord placed me in among the very body of Christ, with a pastor who truly had a heart and a gift for working with extremely broken people with extremely broken lives. Pastor Jeff told me that the Lord was there for me, no matter if I was Walt or Laura, and that He would heal me whoever I was. At his words, hope took root in my soul.

Once I left the women's recovery house, I needed somewhere to stay. Living on my own was not an option financially or emotionally. Someone from church knew a lady named Cathy who was looking for a female roommate. I interviewed with her to rent one of the three bedrooms in her apartment, but I left out the part about being a transsexual. She agreed to rent me the room. As it turned out, Roy knew Cathy from another church. When I told Roy I was moving in with Cathy, he asked me if I had told her my history. I said no.

Well, later that week, I was at work, in the lingerie section of a local department store. When I looked up from the register, I saw Cathy, walking toward me at a fast, very fast pace with a little fire and anger in her eyes. She told me she had talked to Roy, and Roy told her I was once a man. In the best way I could, with no anger, and with a sincere apology for upsetting her, I explained I did not know who to tell and who not to tell.

Immediately, with what I was to learn later was her deep commitment to the Lord and profound compassion for people, she said that my history was okay with her. She wouldn't rent me the room, but I could stay and sleep on the couch temporarily. That was all I had, so I agreed. After about two weeks with me sleeping on the couch and nobody else coming forward to rent the unoccupied bedroom, she had become comfortable enough with me to let me move in and I did.

Back at church, Pastor Jeff enlisted his staff and elders to welcome me, as strange as I appeared, and to offer support both financially and in prayer. Two very significant women on Jeff's staff that loved me more than I loved myself were Dixie Gilbert, Jeff's right hand at church, and Pat Portman, the central hub of all that happened in and around the church.

Pat and Dixie pulled together a group of thirty or so people who pledged their support through money, prayer and love, no matter how long it took, without judging who I should become, but just that I found healing. They committed to pray for my recovery and restoration every week.

My commitment in return was to write a weekly letter to this anonymous (to me) prayer team, which came to be known simply as "the prayer letter." I was to share my most intimate struggles and battles in the prayer letter, no matter how bizarre, uncomfortable, or un-Christ-like they may be, so that the prayer team could pray very specifically for my healing in those areas.

What a catharsis for me! Finally the twisted workings of my mind could be out in the open, without fear. Instead of fleeing into alcohol for relief, I had a safe outlet to reveal and explore the hidden areas that haunted and taunted me. Having so many people truly interested in my healing was inspirational. Jeff's idea for the prayer letter was brilliant and effective for my healing and recovery. God answered the prayers of His saints.

This time of recovery stood in stark contrast to my last failed attempt. This time I was working a rigorous program of AA meetings, and I was embraced by a church's pastor, staff, elders, and committed group of thirty or so people who would support me and read the unvarnished accounts of my weekly battles and successes. All this was due to Pastor Jeff Farrar and his love for working with those with broken lives.

Jeff's Account of Meeting Laura

I was definitely uncertain and nervous when Laura walked into my office. My friend, Roy Thompson, had called and explained her story. I remembered being shocked as I listened to Roy, but then struck by the thought of God's power transforming a person in that situation.

After a few minutes of talking, it became apparent that Laura was more nervous than I. While her story was terribly painful, it dawned on me that from her past experience with other pastors and churches, she expected to be judged and rejected.

I determined to encourage her toward the Lord and Scripture no matter what she had to say. Regardless of her experience and choices, she wasn't too much for the Lord to handle. I also felt strongly that I had little to offer Laura. I told her that I had no experience with her situation. Many of the battles she fought and the choices she faced I had never even thought about let alone encountered. Frankly, I told her, I was afraid that I would do damage to her with any counsel I could come up with. I simply did not know what to say to her.

Laura's answer was, "No one knows what to do with me or say to me. So don't sweat it." One thread through Walt's (then Laura's) life that never changed regardless of the wardrobe, was a tremendous sense of humor. Laura was frank, animated and engaging.

Since it was also apparent she was repentant and broken before the Lord and willing to do whatever she needed to honor Him, I could see no choice but to be available to her.

So began one of the most important and significant relationships in my life. As it was cemented through countless meetings over a number of years, I had found a great friend. Walt/Laura turned out to be a tremendous source of encouragement and model of obedience in the middle of tremendous pain. Watching the miraculous growth from Laura to Walt became my greatest source of confidence that God's power still worked today.

From day one of our relationship, Laura (then Walt) was a great friend, a fellow-soldier in the faith. Walking together through the pain, we cried, trusted and laughed as God led us through this journey. I can say without hesitation that having Walt in my life has been a tremendous gift.

— Jeff Farrar

Chapter 10.
Finding a Career

The department store where I had been working was going out of business. My last weeks there were spent in the china department, packing up the crystal giftware and dishes. I had a year of sober living and my recovery process was stable, thanks to regular attendance at AA meetings, and the accountability that came from writing the weekly prayer letter to the group at church. But I needed to work, and thankfully, the state of California had programs to help me find something. A benefit of having successfully completed a court-ordered recovery program was that the state Department of Rehabilitation would assign a counselor to assist me in my job search. My state counselor was very sensitive to my unusual history and wonderful to work with.

This was 1987 and tolerance for transsexuals in the workplace was non-existent. Back in the days when I was so gung-ho on having the surgery, I had naively blundered ahead, without any thought to how potential employers would react to an applicant who had a job history under both male and female names. Of course, I hadn't thought about it—I hadn't considered the crushing impact on my family either. The only thing driving my decisions at the time was the single-minded pursuit of quieting the lifelong tempest that tossed in my head. Now four years after the deed was done, my incredible ascent up the ladder of success in corporate America was but a memory. My experience and qualifications gained as an executive in the car business were useless in finding present employment. Now that I was sober, I keenly felt the devastating consequences and frustration of being in a mess of my own making. At age 47, my career was washed up, my own poor choices to blame.

Even though I knew I was well-qualified for various state government openings, my applications were denied because I did not disclose that I was a transsexual. How ironic—the same state that issued my new birth certificate declaring that I was a female named Laura Jensen, now claimed "foul" because I didn't say I was a transsexual on the job application. No more chances here—working for the state was out.

My counselor had a list of other companies that regularly hired referrals from the Department of Rehabilitation. I went to every interview she arranged for me—more than fifty interviews in all. Applying for a job as Laura Jensen was a demoralizing and frustrating experience–a real minefield. If I entered "Walt Heyer" under the section "Other Names Used," I had to explain my change from male to female in the interview, a story so bizarre and shocking in those times that it inevitably led to a highly embarrassing and uncomfortable interview, which slammed the door shut on any prospect of a job.

My other unappealing alternative was to leave "Walt Heyer" off the application, get found out, and be denied employment because I had lied on the application. For example, I agonized over my application with United Airlines, whether to put "Walt Heyer" on it or not. After much worrying, I decided to try leaving "Walt Heyer" off the application. They then turned me down for a minimum wage job cleaning airplanes because I omitted it.

Finally, success! Laura was hired. The federal government agency, Federal Deposit Insurance Corporation (FDIC) in San Francisco hired me to operate a photocopy machine. Operating photocopy machines at FDIC was no sit-down job. An extraordinary number of bank failures were occurring in the early 1980s, and each one necessitated the copying of thousands of pages. The anxiety of looking for work was over. I had a solid job with the federal government, working as Laura.

Since I was working in the city, I rented a cheap, tiny studio apartment in the outer Mission District of San Francisco, and Cathy and I parted ways amicably.

I felt re-energized and had a new goal, to be a counselor for alcohol and drug recovery. I started taking night and weekend classes at the University of California Santa Cruz extension campus in Cupertino, about forty-five miles south of the city. My goal was to attain an advanced studies certificate, the first step to becoming an alcohol drug counselor.

By the end of the year, I had finished with all the first-year classes offered in Cupertino. I had done pretty well allocating my time among working days at FDIC in the city, school in the evenings, church and homework on the weekends and AA meetings throughout the week. Even the driving wasn't too bad: ninety miles roundtrip to school during the week, sixty miles roundtrip to church on the weekend.

Now the balancing act that was my life was about to become stretched to the limit. The second-year classes were only available at the main campus in Santa Cruz, about seventy-five miles south of San Francisco. What had been ninety miles roundtrip to classes became one hundred and fifty miles several days a week. I needed more hours in the day. My day job at FDIC wasn't available as a night job, so I transferred to the U. S. Postal Service, sorting mail from 11 p.m. to 6 a.m. at the Rincon Annex in San Francisco. I moved to a bigger and cheaper place in San Carlos, about twenty-five miles south of San Francisco, close to church, and "only" fifty miles to school.

Exhausted from my schedule, I experienced a new level of difficulty in coping. Laura battled for internal control. I was terribly uncomfortable in my own skin. I couldn't find peace no matter how I dressed or acted. I cycled back and forth compulsively, almost without warning, between being Walt and being Laura. Pull off the highway. Take off the dress and put on the slacks. Wipe off the lipstick and comb out my hair. Or vice versa, put on the dress and the lipstick and pouf up my hair. And it didn't stop with appearance. Walt ate junk food; Laura ate healthy food. Walt had a low voice; Laura spoke in a higher pitched range. Walt's handwriting was completely different than Laura's. Even their opinions were different.

I'd be going along as Walt and my mind would buzz with accusations: "You aren't a man—you had surgery. You're a woman now. Look at your birth certificate. It says Laura. What are you doing dressed as a man? That's disgusting!" Or as Laura, the

A TRANSGENDER'S FAITH

opposite thoughts jeered at me: "It's all a masquerade. How can you be a woman? Just because you chopped off your #@*? I don't think so. You were born a man and you are a man. What are you doing with lipstick on? That's crazy." At school and at work I couldn't act on the impulse to change from Laura to Walt without being seen, so I stayed as Laura. But outside of those places, I changed back and forth at will. I went to men's AA meetings as Walt and to women's AA meetings as Laura, but I avoided the mixed meetings. It was too confusing and embarrassing to be caught dressed as the opposite person in public situations.

With the Lord Jesus Christ as my strength, Walt would emerge. Then, overwhelmed with grief and shame at the devastation I had caused my children and myself, I sought escape from the pain and hid in the identity of Laura Jensen. The battle was intense. The girl in the purple dress was winning and Walt was losing.

I realized that if I ever hoped to achieve recovery from the internal battle, the key was sobriety. It became my mantra: "Stay sober—no matter what—stay sober." The prayer letters that I prepared weekly for the support team were effective in holding me accountable in my sobriety and in working through the shame of my past actions.

The group at church did everything to assist me in my recovery and restoration. I stayed connected with those whose support was essential: Roy and his family, Pastor Jeff and the church, and the two Christian psychologists, with whom I met regularly. If I was having trouble coping, so much more so were my supporters. I couldn't adequately express what was happening inside of my mind and the explanations came across as twisted thinking. What my friends saw and experienced were two different personalities, sometimes within moments of the other, with different opinions, different tastes in food, different voice pitch, and different styles of clothing. My inconsistency was mind-blowing. Frustration ran high.

Some church members tried to club me over the head with Bible verses so I would repent of my "sin." A common misconception was that I was addicted to sex or pornography, but I didn't suffer from those issues. For me, pursuing the surgery was motivated by the yearning to fix my identity issue, not by any longing for perverted sex. The hormones killed any desire for sexual relations of any kind. I was totally uninterested.

I persevered in my studies and attained my advanced certificate in drug and alcohol studies at the end of two years, in 1989. I was three years sober, forty-nine years old, ready to use my hard-earned degree. And in my flip-flop fashion, I wanted to be Walt now.

Early the next year, with Roy Thompson's help, I became a drug and alcohol counselor as Walt with CityTeam Ministries in San Jose, California. I was granted a one-year contract at their rehab center, working four days a week with clients. I led group counseling and one-on-one counseling, taught classes, and worked with the state Department of Rehabilitation to help find jobs for the clients who completed the one-year recovery program.

I was now living as Walt and working as Walt. But living alone was tough, too tough. I moved back in with the Thompson family. My contract at CityTeam was for four days a week, so I saw an opportunity to spend the other three days of each week elsewhere. About a two-and-a-half hour drive from the Thompson's Pleasanton home, in the foothills of the Sierra

Nevada, was the beautiful, sleepy little gold rush town of Murphys, California. One of my sponsors from my days at the post office, Tommy O., had a home there and invited me to spend three days a week with his family in Murphys. The small-town Murphys lifestyle was so appealing that I rented a small house next to his family in Murphys.

While hanging out at the newly opened coffee shop on Murphys' Main Street, I came to know the young owners, a husband and wife, as well as with their parents. The entire family adopted me as their own, and became significant links in the chain, a powerful source of modeling of normal relationships and a wellspring of love and friendship that helped to keep me on the path to recovery and restoration.

This was a great combination for my recovery from alcohol. Four days a week, I worked as a counselor in the CityTeam Christian recovery program in San Jose, with Bible study and AA meetings. Three days a week, I spent in Murphys living next-door to my sponsor who had over twenty-five years of sobriety and was extremely active in AA. Coupled with the knowledge I gained through my schooling in alcohol and drug studies from UC Santa Cruz, I was working a vigorous, balanced recovery program to prevent a relapse of drinking. One day at a time. It was working.

Chapter 11.

Invading Laura's Territory

I missed my church family in Foster City. Laura had always been the one to show up at church, and now that I was living full-time as Walt, I avoided weekend services. It would have been too awkward, and Laura would fight me.

But in a moment of confidence, I checked with Pastor Jeff to see if it would be okay for Walt to come to church. The answer to that question from Jeff and the elders resulted in one of the most memorable, supportive days of my life, where I felt the full support of the entire church, cheering me on to resolve my gender conflict. Jeff crafted his entire Sunday message around my story as his way to introduce Walt to the church family who had known me only as Laura.

As Jeff tells it in his own words:

One day Walt called and said he wanted to come back to church. He said God had healed him. Laura was gone and he missed his church. Through all the years of instability, he had only attended as Laura. Obviously this needed careful thought and prayer for its impact on both Walt and the Body.

It was thrilling to hear the change and confidence in Walt's voice but I was fearful that he might be setting himself up for failure if Laura reemerged. I wanted to celebrate with Walt what God had done but wondered if he would be better served by preserving this extended period of stability. My strongest feeling was wanting to protect him.

I told him the elders and I needed to think and pray about it. After discussing it at length, we felt it was most important to honor what God had done in Walt and let the Body share in that. Playing it safe out of fear of reaction or failure seemed a lack of faith.

We selected a Sunday and put much preparation and prayer into it. I preached on God's great love for great sinners. Focusing on the story of Zaccheus, I catalogued how throughout Scripture God has drawn people whose lives were such a mess that no one could have imagined they could be changed. In fact, so often these were God's "chosen."

Then I told Walt's story of abuse, addiction and poor choices, including the tragic step of gender change surgery. The focus was God's great work – changing someone we could never imagine. I wanted them to share in the thrill of a great work God had done and was doing in our midst. Then I introduced Walt.

The response was overwhelming. Every person in the room immediately stood and applauded. It was the most dramatic acknowledgement of God's power I have ever experienced. Then Walt spoke powerfully of God's grace in his life. Standing next to him, I was sobbing openly as were all the elders and the many others who had prayed and stood with Walt through his courageous and painful journey.

I know it went beyond what anyone thought they would encounter in church that day. It went beyond what most imagined could even happen. The reason for the impact that day was that everyone knew that God had done a miraculous work.

Walt says that day had a huge impact on him. Being free to openly celebrate all that God had done launched him forward in his growth and recovery. That day also had a tremendous impact on the church. It affirmed that God was at work among us. It clarified again that the church's priority was being a place of healing amidst the mess of life. It focused us on worshipping the Lord for the great trophy of grace Walt was.

We made it clear that God's work in Walt was far from done. We acknowledged that Walt's experience was far beyond what most of us could understand. But we celebrated as a Body that God had done a miraculous work in our midst. What a great day it was.

—*Pastor Jeff Farrar*

Even though I was receiving immeasurably more support beyond what I could ever imagine, that damn girl in the purple dress continued to try to derail my living as Walt. Walt was working as a counselor at CityTeam in San Jose during the week and "acting out" as Laura in Murphys on the weekends. Why was this happening to me? I did not feel like I was in control all the time of my mind.

I shared this with Roy, with my sponsor, and with my two Christian psychologists. Everyone was just as puzzled as I was. We were all beginning to throw our hands in the air in frustration. I desired to return to the specialist at Stanford who worked with the struggles of transsexuals. She reaffirmed her previous diagnosis that I had the most extreme case of gender dysphoria she had ever seen. And that living as Laura was the answer.

During this struggle I also went to visit the psychologist who originally approved my surgery, Dr. Paul Walker. This was my second visit to confront him since my surgery, seven years earlier. I told him that I had four years of sobriety. This time he confessed that he was also in a 12-step program because at the time that he had approved my surgery, he was addicted to pain killers and alcohol, and now he was sick with AIDS.

Kick me in the stomach. I was stunned. I almost missed his explanation that his addiction to pain killers started with a ski accident and spiral leg fracture. It took me a long time to appreciate the full implication of the news that he was abusing drugs and alcohol when he approved my surgery. A short time after our visit, he wrote me a letter, motivated, I'm sure, by the "making-amends-wherever-possible" step of his 12-step recovery program. In the letter he said, "I assure you that I share, as best I can, some of your pain that this mistake has caused you." Shortly after writing the letter, he died from complications of AIDS. Years later, when I was ready to deal with the piercing pain around the solitary, word "mistake," I was glad to have the letter in my possession.

A TRANSGENDER'S FAITH

May 28, 1990

Dear Walt,

I received your note, forwarded to me by ▓▓▓ ▓▓▓ ▓▓▓▓▓▓.

I was very pleased, for you, in learning of your continued sobriety. I know that the progress towards serenity is often long and painful. Regrets and resentments from the past, it is promised, will eventually leave.

Ever since you last visited me at my office, to tell me that you were thinking of resuming your life as Walt, I have taken every opportunity, at national and international conferences, to warn other therapists of the possibilities of hidden alcohol/drug abuse diagnoses confounding the diagnosis of gender dysphoria. Unfortunately, few traditional therapists have any training in recognizing and treating substance abuse other than in recognizing the obvious terminal-stage "low bottom" liver-failure de-tox center client. Clearly, a lesson from your tragedy is that the alcohol/drug abuse must be addressed first, before the alleged gender issues, assuming that denial does not prevent the chemical abuse from becoming known.

Curiously, it is rather common that gender identity issues are first reported by someone in the course of recovery, having been completely hidden by drugs prior to that. A situation such as yours is, thankfully, unique (that is, where recovery apparently undid the original request for surgery). You will remain always in my prayers.

I have often been criticized throughout my career for being too conservative and too cautious in approving sex reassignment surgery. I had seen too many cases of post-surgical regret, in people treated elsewhere, that I never wanted to have one of the people I had tried to help to ever regret their decision. I assure you that I share, as best I can, some of your pain that this mistake has caused to you.

I know that ▓▓▓ ▓▓▓ ▓▓▓▓▓▓ was seeking information on restoring someone's original birth certificate. If that was for you, let me please offer whatever assistance I can in helping you to correct those records.

I wish you the best of peace and serenity in your future.

Sincerely,

Paul A Walker, Ph.D.

It's no wonder mistakes happen where this surgery is concerned. This may be the only disorder where the patient informs the doctor of the diagnosis and treatment, rather than the other way around. The patient announces he is a woman trapped in a man's body and that declaration, like a golden key, opens the door to having this very radical treatment procedure.

In my case, the psychologist guided me to surgery without first conducting long-term intense psychotherapy that might discover things hidden deep in my psyche that fueled the craving.

Instead of finding out what was driving my desire for surgery, the psychologist invited me to behave and dress as the opposite gender at individual and group therapy sessions. Using that logic to guide a gender disorder patient to recovery is curious. Perhaps the same logic should be applied to the treatment of the alcoholic. We would encourage the alcoholic to get drunk as a way to guide them to recovery. How absurd that would be.

Nothing was helping my gender identity problems. I was in excruciating internal conflict most of the time. It got the best of me and secretly I was cross-dressing. But then, in the eyes of the law of the state of California, was I really cross-dressing? My driver's license and birth certificate said I was Laura Jensen, female. I knew the surgery was all a big mistake, but that didn't help to resolve the turbulence I was experiencing between male and female. Would it ever end?

Walt/Laura talked to therapist after therapist, wanting to discover the magic key. More diagnoses came: severe depression, post traumatic stress disorder, schizophrenia, gender identity disorder. Everyone had an opinion. We researched them all. None of them quite fit. None of these could explain the flip-flopping we were witnessing. We were confused. Walt was confused. Laura was confused.

What a tailspin she experienced. Dissatisfied and restless, Laura again questioned her identity and Walt reappeared. For several years he went from Walt to Laura, Laura to Walt and back again. It was not unusual. There were times we felt that Laura was it, finally permanent. Then Walt would reappear. We could not imagine the confusion and trauma that greeted her every morning.

—Dr. Roy Thompson

Chapter 12.

A Shocking Diagnosis

By 1991, my one-year contract as a counselor was up at CityTeam. Looking for opportunities in my new career, I talked with my old friend and first AA sponsor, Ben, who lived in Los Angeles. He knew of a job opening at a hospital psychiatric ward for dual-diagnosed alcohol and drug patients. It paid well, something I hadn't seen since Honda. The application dilemma—Walt or Laura?—was staring me in the face again. But because my legal documents said "Laura Jensen," I applied for the job as Laura, even though my previous job with CityTeam was as Walt.

I moved into a room in Ben's large Los Angeles house. Having just spent a year working and living as Walt, it was perplexing to me why I was once again making the choice to present myself as Laura Jensen. I was sober and knew the Lord desired for me to stand up and be a man. But that little girl inside me who put on that purple chiffon evening dress at such a young age was still alive, living side-by-side inside of Walt in a very bizarre co-existence, a persona emerging at times and retreating at others. That girl in the purple dress with many names—first named Christal West, then for awhile Andrea West, then starting on the day of surgery, Laura Jensen—again prevailed and took control over Walt, the male. This had been repeated so many times now for so many years, even my most loving good friends were growing weary of it all. Ashamed of my latest failure, my flip-flop back to Laura, I stopped writing the prayer letters to the support team at church.

The job at the medical center psych unit was a good match for Laura. The unit specialized in alcohol drug recovery for patients with severe psychological disorders, from self-mutilation to schizophrenia and hosts of other issues. Working in a hospital environment for twelve-hour shifts as a chemical dependency technician, my duties included taking vital signs, leading group therapy sessions, and developing daily social events, such as walks around the neighborhood and even lunch at a restaurant for patients who were capable of contact with the outside world.

The unit had a fabulous psychiatrist who made rounds on my floor once or twice a day. I thought he was one of the brightest and most fun medical doctors I had ever met, also one of the best-dressed. This M.D. could have graced the cover of GQ magazine with his fashionable appearance: not too tall, not overweight, perhaps in his late forties or early fifties, a class act. He frequently asked for my personal impressions of the behaviors of some of the patients on my unit who were struggling with social interaction with other patients. When he made his rounds, I would answer the questions he had about the patients.

I had been working there about thirty days when this psychiatrist asked me if he could spend time with me, in a clinical environment, with me as the subject. He said it was just to talk with me, providing the staff management gave approval for me to do this. For about three weeks, he asked questions about my life, my struggles, and my surgery. He was interested, very interested. I was amazed that this prominent Beverly Hills M.D. would give his free time just to talk with me. Then he suggested I go for further evaluation with other psychiatrists to be evaluated for a dissociative disorder. I kept silent. I did not know what a dissociative disorder was. He gave me a long list of doctors who could evaluate me and determine if in fact I had a dissociative disorder.

I picked a lady who specialized in dissociative disorder and met with her in her elegantly decorated office on the top floor of a plush Beverly Hills office building for many weeks in order for her to evaluate me. When her evaluation was complete, she called me to come in. Sitting there in her office, she began to tell me I indeed had a dissociative disorder and for the first time, I wanted to know what it meant. She said it was the latest name for multiple personality disorder.

In her view, the combination of the discipline by my mom and dad, the cross-dressing in the purple dress by Grandma, and the molestations by Uncle Fred, all together, were the ingredients for the development of the dissociative disorder, or multiple personality disorder, that I had been suffering from and dealing with all my life. In order to survive, my psyche had split into many pieces, each holding a part of Walt. Furthermore, the surgery was actually performed while I was under the control of what she called a "fragment personality," or an alternate personality, or simply an "alter" who took control of my life from time to time. While the alter was in control, she wanted to eradicate Walt from existence, and having surgery to change gender was how she chose to accomplish it. Unfortunately, the psychiatrist said, having had the surgery would make recovery for Walt very, very difficult.

My head was spinning. Dissociative disorder was a new concept for me, and now two different prominent psychiatrists were seeing in me clear indications of a diagnosis never ever even considered in all my previous counseling. I was at first devastated, and then as I thought about it longer, I wasn't convinced that the specialist was correct. What if her specialty caused her to be predisposed to looking only for multiple personality disorder?

I went to yet another doctor, this time at the Los Angeles Free Clinic, to be evaluated. He was not a specialist and to make his evaluation unbiased, I did not disclose to him what the other two doctors had concluded. After about three sessions, the free clinic doctor came to the same conclusion, just like the two doctors before him: that I had multiple personality disorder.

I started having panic attacks that left me gasping for breath during the night. I just could not grasp the concept that Laura Jensen was a fragment, or an alter personality. How could I continue to live as a fragment person? I wanted to recover but I needed help; I needed extreme counseling.

My GQ psychiatrist suggested I try Prozac, an antidepressant. But within three days of taking it, I told him I couldn't continue. With my history of addiction to drugs and alcohol, often to the brink of death, I couldn't face taking drugs. I had a healthy aversion to using drugs at all, especially as a coping mechanism. It was essential for me to maintain my sobriety, and taking prescription mood-changing drugs seemed like a possible road to relapse for me. I would just have to tough it out without drugs.

With the psychiatrist's help, I found a Ph.D. therapist who specialized in treating dissociative disorder. The first thing the therapist recommended was that I stop indulging the fragment and live life as Walt, not as Laura. That would make keeping my current job, under the name of Laura, difficult. Employers didn't go for people changing genders. After only six months working at the psych unit, I quit my job as Laura, determined to give Walt another chance.

My old friend from American Motors, Bill, was now in management at Toyota, not far from where I was living in Ben's house in LA. Ever since we first developed our friendship twenty-four years before, Bill stuck by me through everything. As he put it, "Walt, Laura, Bozo, whatever you're calling yourself today, you're my friend." I contacted Bill and asked if Toyota had any jobs that I could do. Bill was frank with me: "With your history, there's no way that Toyota will employ you." But he could hire me through a temporary agency to work for a Toyota national recall campaign. I went for it, grateful to be back working with Bill, whom I admired, respected and considered one of my very best friends. Bill was very happy he could help me.

I continued living a dual life: Walt at work, Laura everywhere else. It seemed that Laura was very territorial. If I was introduced to something or someone as Laura, then I felt most comfortable always presenting as Laura in that situation. When I met Ben at my first AA meeting, I was Laura, so I felt most comfortable being Laura living in his home and at the AA meetings. Ben didn't care if I left for work in the morning dressed as Walt. We often laughed and joked about the absurdity of it.

One of Ben's neighbors, who didn't know about my dual identity, asked for his assistance to remove a sliding patio door. I went along to help, and later the neighbor remarked to Ben, "She sure is a strong little thing!" Later as I got to know him, I told him the truth about my birth gender, and the three of us split our sides laughing at his original remark: "She sure is a strong little thing!"

I had tried living a dual lifestyle right after surgery —Walt at work and Laura at home—but extreme consumption of alcohol, combined with my utter ignorance of what troubled me mentally, caused the plan to fail miserably. This time, though, I had sobriety. AA meetings were a very regular thing in my life and my time of recovery now numbered five full years. I was actively working a program of recovery and seeking specialized help for my newly-found diagnosis. My name or gender didn't matter much at the moment.

Oh, how I hated my therapy sessions; they were extremely difficult and very disturbing to my psyche. But I continued to go. I felt like I might finally resolve the 35-year plus battle with the girl in the purple chiffon dress. My Ph.D. counselor said that during sessions conducted under hypnosis, she had identified between thirteen and fifteen separate personalities.

She requested that I bring in anything I had written in my own hand for her to evaluate: notes, journals, any documents with my signature. I had written a lot and I delivered it all. She showed me how each different name had a distinctive signature to go along with it. Andrea signed the consent papers for surgery. "Look here," she said, "Andrea's signature is very tight, small, and left-slanted. Laura's is very bold and slanted the opposite way, to the right."

I was shocked, until I remembered that almost ten years earlier I had noticed the differences but I did not understand what it meant. Now the physical evidence hit me hard, in the face. Staring at the differences in what I knew to be samples of my own handwriting, and remembering the comments from the all the doctors who had suggested a diagnosis of multiple personalities, my denial crumbled and I realized that the diagnosis fit my symptoms. Gender dysphoria was wrong. I suffered from multiple personalities, or dissociative disorder.

For years, I had made decisions about my life based on what I could see now was a misdiagnosis of gender dysphoria, a severe dislike for one's birth gender. I had sought help from the leading specialists, psychologists, and doctors, who urged me to have the extreme surgery as treatment for my disorder. I had had my private parts rearranged, breasts added, and plastic surgeries performed to make my appearance female, which not only failed to give me relief, but quite the opposite, caused me even greater difficulty.

The thought that all this extreme surgery was for nothing blew my mind. I was completely devastated by the realization that the radical treatment I underwent, the surgery recommended by so-called experts, was based on a misdiagnosis. Not only was it unnecessary, it was extremely destructive and had the potential to keep me from ever recovering from my true problem, dissociative disorder.

The ongoing therapy seemed to make my mind more twisted and confused than ever before, like I could not trust myself to know what or who I was. Why was I going through all this stuff?

When would I get some rest? Walt was tired of therapy, tired of being exhausted. This was all very hard work. Like had happened so many times in the past in the midst of difficult situations, the girl in the purple dress wanted to take control and allow Laura Jensen to come back. Here we went again.

In July, 1992, I quit my job at Toyota, stopped the difficult therapy, and looked for a way to move back to the San Francisco Bay Area, back to my church and support team, to be near Roy and his family. I contacted Cathy, the San Francisco Bay Area friend who first rented me a room when I came out of the women's recovery house five years earlier. Cathy loved and cared for people, and I knew she was a safe person to be with. The extra bedroom in her large apartment in Burlingame, close to my church, was available for rent for the next few months. Cathy took me in.

As Laura, I plugged back into the AA meetings I had previously attended and went back to the church where I had had the support team. The Monday after my first weekend back at church, Pastor Jeff called and jarred me with some unexpected news. The elders had met and decided that it was not healthy for the congregation to witness all the changing back and forth I was doing between male and female. As he put it, "I can't tell you not to come here, it's just a request. The elders would appreciate it if you wouldn't come to church here anymore." I was disappointed, but I wasn't angry. I knew seeing me play out my troubles in such a visible, bizarre way made people uncomfortable. And it wasn't Jeff who wanted me gone; he was just relaying the decision of the church elder board.

Two Mondays later, an elder called me. "We are having our weekly meeting and we're calling to tell you we were wrong. This church is a place for broken people. Please come back." Then, one at a time, each elder took the phone to apologize personally to me. As Roy always says, God works both sides of the fence. It was nice to see Him work on the other side for a change.

I selected yet another psychotherapist, this time one near Roy's home who specialized in recovery from dissociative disorder. She determined that working at a normal job was out of the question. I was disabled by the disorder and I would require years of psychotherapy to recover. She suggested that I take my written diagnoses from all the doctors and use them to apply for permanent disability under the federal Supplemental Security Income (SSI) program. SSI is designed to help aged, blind, and disabled people, who have little or no income. It provides cash to meet basic needs for food, clothing, and shelter.

The one-year waiting period for the start of SSI disability income was a tough one. My psyche was unsettled by the intensive therapy and my financial situation was dismal. The temporary disability payment from the state was a meager one.

And yet miracles happened along the way. A man I met through my Bay Area sponsor, Tommy O., was so touched by my story that he changed his will to leave me his old pickup truck and camper shell. After his friend died and I received the truck, Tommy gave me lots of ribbing about how his long-time friend left him nothing, but to me, whom he barely knew, he bequeathed his truck. In my destitute state, I considered the old pickup and camper shell to be a godsend.

The family in Murphys who owned the restaurant allowed me to run errands in exchange for meals at the restaurant. In an act of incredible generosity, they set aside a room in their home for me, so I wouldn't have to spend the cold Murphys winter nights in the unheated camper. They loved me, never pressured me, and always included me with the family. They entrusted me to baby-sit for their young daughter.

During the year, I alternately lived in the Bay Area at Cathy's or with the Thompson's, and in Murphys with Tommy O. and his family, or with the restaurant owners, or in the camper, barely scraping by. Being on the receiving end of the generosity of others was a humbling experience, but to survive, I accepted it with thanks.

Time with these families made me feel normal. Being surrounded by real men and real women in normal living situations helped me see how wrong my masquerade was. Healthy relationships, seen up close, have enormous positive impact to a broken person.

After the SSI waiting period was over, I began drawing permanent disability income, which enabled me to focus on my recovery and less on survival. Somewhere during this time, my daughter tentatively allowed me back into her life. It was a start.

I don't remember much from the sessions with the psychotherapist who specialized in recovery from dissociative disorder. They say that's part of the disorder—missing pieces in one's memories. I remember more from the sessions with the Christian psychologists because it was less invasive and focused on more "normal" things, such as childhood issues and maintaining my sobriety.

For one session, I prepared my personal inventory, a requirement of working the 12-step program's fourth step. Most people write a few pages, maybe ten, to identify resentments, pain, and unresolved issues of their past that they are ready to turn over to their higher power. My account was over a hundred pages long. The therapy session lasted four hours, ending with us in the parking lot, where we burned the pages, to symbolically let the pain and resentments go.

As the ashes were smoldering and a gentle breeze lifted them upward, I felt a strong sense of relief and lightness, as if my heart had been liberated from a heavy weight. My psychologist and I returned inside to his office for prayer. As he prayed for me, I had a very personal encounter with Jesus, a powerful spiritual experience. In my vision, the Lord was dressed all in white, with His feet hidden under His robe. As He approached me with his arm stretched out and a generous smile on His face, I saw myself as a baby. At that very moment, he scooped me up and said, "You are now safe with me forever." I was in His arms and together we were moving upward. Then the vision was over. Tears streamed down my cheeks, a smile on my face.

I do not remember what words my therapist prayed on that special day, but I sure remember my face-to-face encounter with the Lord and His words, "You are now safe with me forever." I would recover—I knew that for sure now.

Walt brought an incredible gift of laughter to our home. He had a tremendous capacity to joke about his experience. It was a welcome relief valve. Many times our laughter was so deep it brought us to tears.

And perseverance. Walt and Laura continued to journal, and to seek help, spiritually and emotionally. His desire for wholeness never ceased.

Multiple personality disorder, or dissociative disorder as it is now called, was the key. The other diagnoses did not fit because they were wrong. Hope at last. All the pieces were falling in place.

WALT HEYER

Finally, the bright light at the end of a very long tunnel. Walt spent another year in therapy integrating the personalities and peace came as a welcome guest to his soul.

—*Dr. Roy Thompson*

Chapter 13.

In the Arms of the Lord

Finally I was at peace. I knew that recovery and restoration would come. The Lord was holding me in His arms.

To qualify for federal permanent disability, a new group of doctors evaluated me and required me to perform a series of written and oral exams. They concluded that I suffered from dissociative disorder and subsequently I was placed on permanent disability. With that resolved, I received shelter in federal housing and a check each month. Now I was free to pursue therapy treatment for my disorder with an open-ended time frame.

The therapy continued, my AA meetings continued, my faith in the ability of Christ to restore me grew. It was only a question of how long it would take. And then there was the issue of my legal identifying documents. My birth certificate still said female and my driver's license was issued to Laura, female. I still had major obstacles to overcome on the difficult road to restoring my male identity.

I clung to the revelation that Dr. Walker had made in his letter the year or so before: "I assure you that I share, as best I can, some of your pain that *this mistake* has caused to you" (italics mine).

Seeing the word "mistake" in a letter from the expert who approved me for surgery gave me an important piece of truth which began the healing in my innermost being. The surgery was all a mistake, performed as treatment for a disorder I didn't have. I wasn't a man trapped in a woman's body. I was an alcoholic with dissociative disorder trying to escape the pain of my childhood. I continued my intensive therapy, drew close to Jesus Christ and my church family, and stayed sober no matter what.

That didn't mean it was easy for me. The five years from 1992 through 1996 were very difficult. I was back on the yo-yo of bouncing between living as Walt and then Laura, changing jobs each time I changed persona.

I found work as a salesman at an oil company thanks to a friend, Patrick, who also worked there. The job didn't last, but months later Patrick called with a proposal. He wanted to start a trucking company hauling gasoline and he wanted me to go in with him. We incorporated the company, got a checking account and started looking for rental property for a small office and space to keep two or three gasoline trucks. A long-time friend of Patrick's lent him $190,000.

We were only weeks away from opening when a friend from church called to say that Patrick had placed a plastic bag over his head and suffocated himself because of a failed relationship with a long-time girlfriend. Again, as a coping response, I switched to being Laura and found a job in a coffee shop.

During this five year period, several of my closest personal friends and supporters died. My great friend, Jon Thompson, who waited for me at the bus stop in his wheelchair when I was living with him and his family in Pleasanton, was diagnosed with AIDS. This dreadful illness was transmitted to him through a blood transfusion done years before, before the medical community was aware of the need to test the blood supply. He had been paralyzed in a freak accident at age nine—hit by a car while standing on the sidewalk. That was tragedy enough, but now suddenly at twenty-nine years of age, he was gone, a casualty of someone else's illness transmitted through the public blood supply.

My long-time counselor, Dr. Dennis Guernsey, was diagnosed with brain cancer and died shortly after my last visit with him. Then Cathy, who gave me my first place to stay after leaving the recovery house, was diagnosed with colon cancer at age forty-six. The growth wasn't discovered until well after it had spread throughout her internal organs. She lost weight fast and was hospitalized frequently. During that time, large numbers of Cathy's friends surrounded her to offer support, including me.

Most of Cathy's friends knew me and my story. If I hung around with anyone long enough, it became awkward to keep the secret. With my permission, Cathy told her close friend, Kaycee, about my surgery and my switching back and forth between Laura and Walt. It did not seem very important to her. That was good for me, to have another person who knew and accepted my past, someone who was safe.

Cathy, Kaycee, and I went out for a meal together every once in awhile. Now with Cathy being so sick, Kaycee and I started getting together more and more to have coffee and to lean on each other in order to cope with Cathy's terminal illness. The Lord was at work, pulling us together in a time of great difficulty. He was revealing His plan for my recovery and restoration and the key was Kaycee. She just didn't know it yet. And I couldn't quite grasp the wild idea that God could or would restore that part of my life.

Relationships were extremely important to me. They helped me feel like a normal person. I maintained continuous contact throughout the years with Pastor Jeff, who rallied together a healing support team from my church; with Bill, my great friend from my American Motors days and his wife; with my sponsors from AA, Tom, Ben and Michael; with Ed, the body shop owner who never gave up on me; and with my son, who had always been my best friend. My son even went to work at Ed's body shop after high school to be close to me. The ladies at church, Pat and Dixie, were constant and continuous support, as well as Roy Thompson and his family. They all believed that the Lord was powerful enough to heal me.

Even though I was on permanent SSI disability and living in federal housing, I knew the Lord wanted me to trust Him with my life, and not to depend on government handouts. So I contacted my good friend Ed once again for a job as Walt. Ed was on the board of directors of a machine shop in the Bay Area and he used his influence in late 1996 to get me a job starting as a delivery driver, with the promise of advancement. This was cool and a great fit for me as Walt. I moved out of the federal housing for the permanently disabled in Murphys and back in with the

Thompson's in Pleasanton. Ten years after I first arrived at the Thompson's, I was back one more time.

Living back in the Bay Area allowed me to visit more with Cathy as she continued to battle colon cancer. I hated being in hospitals, so I'd convince her friend Kaycee to go with me to visit Cathy during the times when she needed to be hospitalized. The Lord was using this friend's illness to draw Kaycee and me together in a way only the Lord can do.

This "Walt" thing was taking hold. I wanted my appearance to be as male as it could be. Some of the cosmetic procedures could not be undone, but the implants could come out, so I had them removed. It felt like the right time to attempt to have that key piece of legal identification, my amended birth certificate, restored from Laura female to Walt male, my true name and birth gender. The court had turned down my petition in 1990, saying that I needed an affidavit. Now seven years later, I was emotionally ready to try again.

I found another attorney and together we developed our strategy. We would appear in court with an affidavit prepared by a surgeon stating that I was a male. The affidavit would be written very strongly, leaving no question about my gender being male. I was sure we would prevail.

Unfortunately the law in California for changing the gender on a birth certificate specified a one-way trip. The laws in place would not permit a birth certificate to be changed back without more surgical procedures, many more surgical procedures. The cost and risk of the surgery was out of the question for me. For now, the door to restoring my birth certificate was closed.

I was falling hard for Kaycee. She seemed more cautious. But motivated by the possibilities, I desperately wanted my legal identity to be Walt Heyer, male, even without a restored birth certificate. There must be something else I could do. I racked my brain trying to devise other strategies that might work. I had my affidavit from the doctors. What other items of identity could I change back to Walt without having a birth certificate? I could register to vote as Walt. The Social Security Administration was willing to change my name back to Walt. I could get a new driver's license. Step by step, I built up a portfolio of documents in the name of Walt, my birth identity.

The next hurdle was my passport; it still said Laura. The pain of using it a year ago in the presence of my son at his Air Force base in England still cut deep. I had always been Walt with my children. I had never allowed them to witness me dressed or acting as Laura. But when we stopped at the guardhouse to present our credentials, my son saw that my passport had the name of Laura Jensen, with the matching picture. His pain, embarrassment and anger were evident, and it upset him for the rest of the visit. I needed to try to amend the identity on my passport.

With the voter registration, doctors' affidavits, driver's license, Social Security card, passport photo and application clutched tightly in my hand, I waiting in the long line at the downtown San Francisco passport office—San Francisco, where anything goes. Finally it was my turn. I had the driver's license issued to Walt Heyer, male, and the Social Security card issued in the name of Walt Heyer. This was the big test. Were they enough?

I gave the items to the man at the window. When he researched my Social Security record, it showed me as Walt Heyer, <u>female</u>. This was just awful. The man at the window said that he could not give me a passport with a male identity. I could have a passport as Walt Heyer, female. How crazy is this? Destroying my real identity after surgery had been so easy. Restoring it back was proving to be seemingly impossible.

As I calmly as I could, I asked if I could see his supervisor. A tall, slender, older woman walked to the window. "I'm the supervisor. How can I help you?" she said. With a quivering voice and trembling hands, I spoke very slowly, even haltingly. It was hard to breathe or catch my breath. I slowly unfolded the documents and told her my long story and how important it was to me to have a passport showing Walt, male. I was almost in tears when she gently laid her hand on top of mine and said, "Sweetie, I'm going to take care of this for you. You will have your passport as Walt Heyer, male. Don't you worry. This needs to be done."

And so it was. That angel at the passport office did what the judge did not—restored my identity to Walt Heyer, male. I may never get my birth certificate itself to read correctly, but the passport works just as well.

The Lord was clearly fulfilling His promise to take care of me. Only He could have influenced the supervisor at the passport office to have such favor on my request. Only He could have painstakingly brought me through the elongated, painful, tangled, and convoluted process to heal my thinking and desires about my gender such that Ed would take another chance on me, and recommend me for a job that held the promise of a new career.

December of 1996 held the promise of exciting new opportunities: with a promising new job for Walt and an unexpected invitation from Kaycee to attend her employer's Christmas party. Picking Kaycee up in my car, I was a little awkward at first, being out with a woman, but she assured me that we were "just buddies." I'm not sure that was what I wanted to hear. We were getting to be close friends, able to confide in each other about our personal struggles and to pray for our very sick friend, Cathy.

I was starting to believe in miracles—even I could not deny that the tide of trouble was beginning to turn. What a string of amazing developments: my passport now issued in the name of Walt—male, my exciting new opportunity at the machine shop, and the joy of developing a relationship with Kaycee. My little feet could not stay on the ground.

My new friend Kaycee was a computer "geek." I was not. Working at the machine shop I was able to afford a used Apple laptop computer and found a wireless Internet service called "Ricochet." It was cutting-edge technology in a time when wireless networks didn't exist. By attaching a little box to the laptop, you could send and receive email anywhere in the Bay Area. It was dial-up service, without being tethered to a telephone. I was able to drop an email to Kaycee when I was in a coffee shop (I did that frequently) or during my lunch hour, sitting in my car. It was fun, talking throughout the day by email.

After the Christmas party, I discovered that Kaycee's birthday was in mid-January, so I called her and asked if I could take her to dinner on her birthday. To my joyful surprise she said yes. We enjoyed a wonderful dinner, laughed and talked. After paying the bill, I stood up to go, but she stayed seated. She looked up at me with a jaunty smile and said, "Do you know what you just did?" Alarmed and befuddled, thinking I must have committed some grievous error, I sat back down and asked, "No, what did I do?"

A TRANSGENDER'S FAITH

She replied, "You just did a date!" Then we both howled with laughter.

I tried to see Kaycee every few days for coffee—as I said, I was falling hard. We went to a movie and I took the chance of a lifetime and, feeling like a teenager, placed my hand gently over her hand and hung on for dear life. It was electric. By February 6, we were both aware that the Lord was weaving us together and we had our first hug. Then on February 8, our first kiss. (Like a teenager, I kept notes in my calendar.) On Valentine's Day, dinner and dancing.

I had not been in any relationship of any kind, not even a date, for fifteen years—since my first marriage ended. My life had revolved around staying sober. My social life was attending AA meetings and church. I had no desire for romantic involvement. I was far too depressed through the years after surgery to have any desire to become involved in romantic relationships. Switching back and forth between Walt and Laura made it impossible to even consider having other relationships. I wasn't homosexual. I never had been. The only love interest I ever would have wanted would be for a woman, but my view of myself through those years was that I was on the trash heap of humanity—someone no one would ever want.

A miracle was unfolding in this area of my life that I had thought was beyond redemption. Kaycee was making me feel different about myself. Only the Lord could have begun this weaving of two very different lives together. There was an undeniable explosion of love. You cannot explain it. You can't understand it, but you sure can feel it, and there is nothing like it. I knew it was love, the love the Lord places on your heart for one special lady like Kaycee.

On February 16, we drove to the Los Angeles area to introduce Kaycee to my daughter and to my mother. As the visit ended and we were saying our final good-byes, my daughter whispered in Kaycee's ear, "Thanks for taking care of my dad." This struck me as an amazing acknowledgment of my daughter's desire to see me restored. Another miracle.

On February 18, at a candlelight dinner at Kaycee's, she expressed a desire to have me as her "boyfriend", with the Lord as our guide. Now my feet were totally unable to touch the ground. By now I had known Kaycee off and on for almost five years. I knew her strength, like mine, was in the Lord. We were going to do this courtship the Lord's way.

Roy and Bonita didn't try to hide their approval, with remarks such as: "Our backyard makes a terrific setting for a wedding." I met Kaycee's friends and went to several counseling sessions with her Christian counselor. Kaycee wanted everyone to get to know her new beau, and to affirm her choice.

On Easter Sunday, I asked Kaycee if she would consider marrying me, and she said yes. The date was set for May 18, only six weeks later. We quickly started the pre-marital counseling program that Kaycee's pastor required, which included taking tests to evaluate our compatibility and maturity for marriage. We scored off the charts to his surprise and our delight. We were giggly, dreamily, and rip-roaringly joyous together as we planned our wedding day celebration.

In the Thompson's garden, on an unseasonably warm May afternoon, we were married by Roy Thompson and Kaycee's pastor, who shared the officiating duties. Best man was Jeff Farrar, the brilliant pastor who encouraged a whole congregation to support me during hard times. Maid of honor was Cathy, dear friend to both of us, ill with cancer, and as it turned out, less than two months from going home to the Lord. In attendance were all the members of the formerly secret prayer team, church elders, our families and loving friends who walked with me from brokenness to wholeness. Truly this was the Lord's day and His blessings were written in every smile on every face.

Only God could have placed a woman in my life that was my perfect soul-mate, allowing us to be friends first, and then weaving us together in marriage. What a joyous day it was, May 18, 1997, in the Thompson's garden in Pleasanton, joining our lives together in marriage in the presence of my approving and cheering pastors, friends, and faithful supporters.

To the glory of God, my struggle with identity was over and a new life began. I am the man God created me to be.

Even though Walt and Kaycee faced unusual issues in beginning a life together, they had a great head start by knowing that marriage is a commitment of a man and a woman to each another, and both to Jesus Christ. And it did happen—to Walt's absolute amazement! In our backyard, in front of a hundred guests, we had the wedding of a lifetime. God in His "more than you could ever ask or think" way, provided Walt with an amazing companion named Kaycee. To watch their love for each other grow is a marvelous reminder that God's grace is alive; it is sufficient; it is beyond our understanding!

—Dr. Roy Thompson

Chapter 14.

A Love Story—by Kaycee

When our mutual friend Cathy shared with me the nature of Walt's struggle, I was shocked—I had never heard of anyone having this kind of surgery, or this kind of problem. Even though I really didn't know Walt, my heart went out to him.

I tended to gravitate toward people who weren't perfect, people who had struggled through complex issues and come out the other side, people with life wisdom gained the hard way. My own maturing process had been a struggle, with years of therapy required to learn how to "be". My marriage of thirteen years ended in divorce, which, while done in a "civilized" manner, was painful. I had no children, just me and like single women everywhere, my cat. And I had a big plus: a new relationship with God, specifically Jesus Christ.

Having been single for several years already, I was determined to focus first on my relationship with Jesus Christ and second, on learning how to form healthy relationships. With the assistance of a counselor I doggedly pursued any hurts or hang-ups that held me back emotionally. As a result, I liked being with people who had experienced gut-wrenching pain and done the hard work of therapy like I was doing. They were real, and they didn't make me feel like I was the "odd" one.

Immediately, my heart warmed to Walt and his struggles. I had never known anyone who had battled and overcome so much, particularly with something as basic and essential as one's gender. Over the course of many conversations with Walt over several years, I became familiar with his world, one filled with the tragic unforeseen consequences of earlier choices.

When Cathy and I would meet Walt for an occasional breakfast, I'd hear his frustration spill out about his menial job, or at other times, his lack of job. I got used to hearing him say: "If only someone would give me a chance. I can do so many things." How he had so much more to give than baking muffins at a coffee shop. How he hated not making a living wage and having to depend on others for life's necessities. I was naive—why couldn't he get a good job and keep it? It sounded like just so much whining to me. Then he'd explain how the sections on the job application that were no problem for someone like me, loomed large for Walt whose job history bounced back and forth between two different names and genders. It was a minefield with no clear path through. I kept thinking that, with all his talents, Walt should work for himself, in his own business, but I didn't push it. He was single-mindedly determined to be accepted back into the corporate world.

Walt was Cathy's friend, so if the three of us got together, it was her idea. But Walt would insist on paying for our lunch. He didn't live close by, but rather than inconvenience us with the driving, he would insist on driving over to our side of the Bay. I was starting to feel an imbalance in our friendship. Due to my own bent toward co-dependency I was very much on alert about keeping a sense of equity in the effort of my friendships. It bugged me because I knew he was barely making ends meet. I needed to do something for him.

One Saturday afternoon, I picked up some burritos and drove to meet him at Ed's shop twenty-five miles away, where he was restoring a truck. He was blown away that anyone would drive so far to bring him lunch. We later referred to it as "the burrito experience." Walt says that's when he started to fall for me.

It's hard to remember the specifics of how our friendship grew, because it was so gradual and natural, never forced. I just knew he was easy to be with. It was a little bit like the taming of the fox in *The Little Prince* by Antoine de Saint Exupéry. Walt was a little skittish and months would pass without seeing him. Now with hindsight, I know that those were the "Laura" times.

When Walt rented his own apartment in a nearby town, Cathy suggested that we get some gifts and celebrate his ability to afford his own place. He proudly showed off his apartment, effusing over the generous gifts from a house-warming party given in his honor the week before by his supporters. The living room, sparsely furnished with one easy chair and a television, seemed a little lonely to me.

I've always been very conservative and practical in the cars I acquire. I kept my first car for ten years, and the second one for eight years. But all the counseling was having a freeing effect on me. When I saw a red convertible advertised at work, I decided to buy it. However, because I'm very practical and it was a used car, I wanted someone to check it over for me first. Cathy recommended that I call Walt—he was good with cars. On the phone I described the three-year-old Toyota Celica convertible with only 17,000 miles on it and asked if he would look it over for me. He was so funny: "That's a new car! Buy it!" With his encouragement, I became the proud owner of a bright red convertible.

It only seemed right that I show Walt the car. He had been so encouraging. After that our friendship grew, and I made sure that I always knew Walt's phone number, no matter where he moved—whether briefly at the apartment, or back at the Thompson's, or in Murphys, or in San Diego. I counted him among one of very few people that I totally trusted and could talk to about anything.

Then in the spring of 1996, at the age of 46, Cathy was diagnosed with terminal cancer. When I didn't know what to do or what to say to my best friend, I could count on Walt's wisdom. I so appreciated his friendship. We even prayed together; healing for Cathy, a job for Walt, and for me, a husband!

In December, I suggested to Walt that he and I do something fun together. We were always dwelling on Cathy's illness, how about a movie? He was living in Pleasanton with the Thompson's, and I again felt that he was doing all the driving in our friendship, so I insisted on driving the forty or so miles to Pleasanton. Afterwards, he took me to meet Bonita and Roy Thompson for the first time.

Bonita delights in telling the story of how she invited me to sit down, and rather than taking the empty single chair, I cleared the things off the loveseat next to where Walt was already sitting. Months later Walt told me that after I left Bonita told him, "Watch out. She really likes you. She could have taken a seat anywhere, but she moved the laundry to sit next to you. Trust me; I'm never wrong about these things." Bonita was hearing wedding bells and Walt and I hadn't even had a real date yet.

I only knew that I loved being with Walt. He was easy to be with. When I needed someone fun to go with me to my company's lavish Christmas party, I thought Walt would be perfect. I knew he would be appropriate and yet playful. At the entrance to the party, the coat-check clerk asked if we were a couple, and I quickly assured the clerk we were not a couple, just "buddies". Walt kidded me all night, "He only wanted to know whether to put the coats on the same ticket or not."

At Christmas time, when Walt insisted on taking me to the airport to catch my flight to see my family, and to pick me up when I returned, eighty miles round-trip from his home at the Thompson's in Pleasanton, I began to think maybe he was getting sweet on me. Then he asked me out for my birthday, three weeks away. No friend had ever reserved my birthday that many weeks ahead. It started to dawn on me that Walt wanted to date, not just be friends.

I wanted to do everything in this relationship Christ's way, not my way. After eight years of being single and eight years of growing in my knowledge of Jesus, I had come to learn that I could only marry a man that fit the biblical description of a godly husband. And I wanted to make very sure Walt was that man before committing my heart to him, even for dating. I knew that if I were to toy with Walt's affections and date him without being open to the possibility of marriage, I would hurt him deeply when we parted ways. It was written all over his face. I did not want to inflict that kind of harm on my precious friend.

For the previous five or so years, with the assistance of an incredible Christian counselor, I had worked on resolving my childhood issues, growing in God's way of being single and developing healthy relationships. With her guidance a year earlier, I had developed a wish list of attributes that my ideal mate would possess. The lineup of traits was wide-ranging—39 items—and included such things as: pleasant attitude, kind to all, loves Jesus, laughs at himself, laughs with me, has close friends, gets over arguments easily, romantic, been through a small crisis and come out the other side, and so on. It was no surprise to me that Walt had 38 out of 39 items! Everyone always asks: "What was the other one?" I'll tell you—it was skiing. Right then and there I decided I could be happy in life without ever skiing again.

In the light of such overwhelming evidence that Walt was God's answer to my prayers, I arranged for him to meet my counselor. With his permission, I shared his history with her privately so she could give her honest opinion of us based on knowing everything. After spending time with us together, seeing us interact and answering her questions, she expressed her delight with the match-up. Later she told me that she could see that the Lord would use each of us to complete the healing in the other. And that has proven to be so very true. Unconditional love is a powerful healing force.

Of course Walt and I had to discuss the very important physical issues. I asked Walt, "Does it matter to you that I'm taller than you?" He answered, "No, does it bother you that I'm shorter than you?" And that simple declaration was the end of any concern about my being two inches taller. And in that same simplicity of heart, with God's grace, and through our mutual unconditional love, other differences that might have mattered a great deal have mattered not at all.

Walt was embarrassed that his chest bore the scars of previous surgeries. My response was that all people get scarred in life; he just happened to have his scars on the outside. They didn't matter to me. His scarred chest is simply a reminder of how fierce the battle was that he had waged most of his life. Since our wedding, we have developed an easy way of relating, and we complement the strengths and weaknesses of one other. Walt is the visionary and I'm the detailed task-master. Some of the most satisfying times in our marriage have been those when we worked together on a project.

For example, we developed our own self-storage business from the ground-up. Walt's business instincts, honed during his car-business days, gave him the vision for where and what the business could be. My business degree and career in the computer industry gave me a sense for the practical details of budget and financing, and the computer needs. We spent months working together to make the vision a reality. It was extremely satisfying to see the business succeed due to our efforts, and the experience gave us a deeper appreciation and love for the other.

In our eight years of marriage, I've seen Walt "kick so much old baggage down the hill." Roadblocks that formerly stood in his way have disappeared through his hard work and determination to try. I always thought he'd do well in his own business, and he proved me right! He later sold our successful self-storage business at a profit. Then he bought a "fixer-upper" condo and completely gutted and updated it, with stunning results.

One accomplishment that eluded Walt during his early years of recovery was to successfully gain employment with a major corporation, even if it was only an entry-level position. He was reluctant to try due to the many painful rejections in the past. But when a major hotel chain in our area held a job fair to solicit employees for their new timeshare resort, I encouraged him to go and submit his application. It would be a tell-tale sign whether or not his past history still blocked his way. Imagine our celebration when Walt was selected for guardhouse duty at the entry gate, a full-time job with benefits! Even though advancement in the hospitality industry is not something Walt desired, recovery from the past is measured in such small steps.

Laboring together on this book has been very fulfilling. Walt wrote while I edited and organized it. We've felt the Lord's blessing as we've pushed through to the finish. My prayer is that the Lord will show you how to apply the truths found here to expand your own heart's capacity to love the people God has placed around you, and to never lose trust that God will answer your prayers.

Love never gives up, never loses faith, is always hopeful, and endures through every circumstance.
(1 Corinthians 13:7, New Living Translation)

God can do anything, you know—far more than you could ever imagine or guess or request in your wildest dreams! He does it not by pushing us around but by working within us, his Spirit deeply and gently within us.
(Ephesians 3:20 The Message Bible)

Chapter 15.

Epilogue 2005

Once again I'm on a plane over Denver, Colorado. At the beginning of this story, I was on a flight to Denver, too, but now over twenty-four years later, my life is very different.

Appropriately, this time I am leaving Denver behind. It's the day after Christmas, 2005, and Kaycee and I are on the second leg of our trip returning from a wonderful Christmas spent with my son, his wife, and the grandchildren. I look out on the night scene from the window of our plane and see the Christmas lights sparkling like fine gemstones on black velvet. The headlights of vehicles can be seen moving about on the roadways around Denver.

I realize I have come full circle in the past twenty-four years. The 1981 flight was where secrecy, deception, and lies prevailed, which ultimately brought me and my family excruciating pain and great confusion.

This flight in 2005 is very different. My wife of almost nine years, Kaycee, is at my side. I am close to having twenty continuous years of clean and sober living. And we just enjoyed a wonderful Christmas with family where the only gift I requested was Eugene Peterson's *The Message Bible*. Comparing the fullness and joy in my life now with the destructive events of the past, I can truly say: "I traded my sorrows."

Now, at the start of a new year, 2006, some thirteen years after that initial diagnosis of dissociative disorder, Kaycee and I have celebrated over eight years together in a really fun marriage. I can tell you this—the Lord's power to heal is more powerful than I could have ever dreamed. My thoughts of gender switching are gone and have been for nearly ten years. The past is like a nightmare from which I finally awoke.

As you have read, it was a bit of a wild ride until I understood the diagnosis of dissociative disorder, a.k.a. multiple personality disorder. As troubling as it was to hear that this strange mental disorder had been playing with my good judgment for most of my life, I was relieved because it felt like it fit—I was comfortable with the diagnosis.

The message of hope was advanced throughout the years of my adult life by a divergent cast of characters with an unlikely mixture of views, but with an underlying theme held in common: a sense of caring for this lost person. Each person who invested time and energy in my recovery, in his or her own individual way, delivered an important, significant and powerful piece of the message that ended up transforming my life. Some people gave up on me, but that was all part of God's plan too.

My hope is that by seeing all the messages and the messengers here, strung together like links in a chain, you will sense the significance of each person to my journey to healing. There are no accidental or insignificant encounters where God is concerned. God had his hand on me, directing me on the road to restoration. And God used people, in my case, many people, to work out his healing for just one person, me.

Having Kaycee as my wife is a gift from Jesus Christ himself. The effect of this tremendous gift cannot go unnoticed by me or anyone who knows my story. She loves me, I mean she loves me so much as Walt, the only personality and person she knew. The events that were in the past were just that—in the past. Kaycee said to me one time, "That 'baggage' of yours, just kick it over the cliff and down the hill. It's gone." She was right. During the time of developing our friendship, when I was concerned whether I could hold Walt together, she made a profound statement, "What's the matter? Don't you think your God is big enough to heal you?"

Kaycee knew the Lord and she knew me better than I knew me. She was correct. I have not had even a ripple of twisted thinking or gender switching. Looking back, it is like it happened to someone else. Well, go figure! That's the multiple personalities. It *was* someone else, or at least a fragment of a personality.

My sobriety, now numbering almost twenty years, is a major element of my daily life. I have enjoyed over ten continuous years of good mental health—truly the Lord has restored me. I have never been more "free and clear" and sound of mind than I am today.

Both my daughter and my son are very much in my life today and there is no overestimating the power of their love in my healing and restoration. My daughter, who justifiably felt very angry and betrayed by me during her teen years, came back into my life after she could witness some longevity in my recovery. Reconnecting with her was very healing and significant. She and her husband join us for Thanksgiving, birthdays, and for no occasion at all.

Each morning and night, and at times in between, Kaycee and I pray together and thank the Lord for the blessings he piles on us each and every day. Blessings like the fabulous relationship I have with my son, his wife and their children. We frequently visit and spend time together, making a special effort to be with each other at Christmas.

The Lord amazes me in his attention to detail. Two years ago, our church was without a senior pastor and needed one to preach for the interim period. Imagine my goose-bumps when I heard that the person selected was someone I knew, but I hadn't seen or talked to in twenty years, Bob Kraning. Bob Kraning, whom I had gotten to know some thirty years earlier at Forest Home Christian Conference Center, and who had worked so hard in vain to prevent my disaster. What would he think now?

I alerted him ahead of time via email that he would see me at the church and tried to fill in the gaps since he had last seen me. I expressed my delight at being able to visit with him and his wife Carol once again, only this time he would see first-hand the restoration the Lord had done in my life. When Bob received my email, he immediately picked up the phone and called me. He was very curious and eager to hear how everything turned out. In typical Bob fashion, he remembered and asked about the rest of my family. He and I made a date to get together with our wives after that weekend's Saturday service.

A TRANSGENDER'S FAITH

I went early that Saturday night. I was nervous, with sweaty palms, my senses a little on edge, since I had not seen Bob for over twenty years. In the dimly lit sanctuary I waited. About a hundred feet away, I saw the backlit figure of a man walking from the bright sunshine into the darkened room. The silhouette was unmistakably Bob Kraning walking directly toward me. He didn't recognize me. In a friendly fashion, he stuck out his hand and said, "Hi, I'm Bob Kraning." "I'm Walt Heyer," I replied, and we fell into a big bear hug of recognition, love and tears. Bob knew I was an incredible living example of the power, love and grace of Jesus Christ who restores broken lives.

As we sized up the changes twenty years had wrought in the other's appearance, the first thing I said was, "Bob, I was a little screwed up the last time you saw me." Bob in a louder than normal voice, with a jaunty smile, replied, "Ya think?!" For months, Kaycee and I responded to everything and anything with Bob's rendition of "Ya think?!" and it never failed to make us laugh. It was so perfect a response on his part, and put me at ease.

Bob Kraning is God's man. He is what God designed a godly man to be. His wife is equally a godly woman. Together they make a wonderful couple who are a joy to be around. The gift of my sixty-third birthday was to celebrate it with Bob and Carol over dinner. What serendipity—encountering those two people who were so pivotal in earlier, painful times of my life, and having the opportunity to show them how my life had been restored. I will always mark this as a miraculous event in my life.

While there were many counselors throughout my long journey, two stood out. Dr. D., a psychologist, who from the time I first arrived at the Thompson home provided very strong, confronting counseling on one hand and loving guidance and support with the other: a balance that worked. The second psychologist was Dr. Jonathan "Sunny" Arnold, a friend of Pastor Jeff Farrar, who helped specifically with my switching back and forth between Laura and Walt.

The families in the rural town of Murphys protected me, loved me, fed me and housed me during the difficult financial and emotional times. Their deep caring was consistent no matter how confused I was. They allowed me to see what normal was, and they gave me a home away from home, a quiet place to rest. Together we still laugh and cry remembering the past. We marvel together at what God has done to restore my life. Our heart bonds run deep.

Surprising to me is the core group of my high school buddies who have walked through every step of the way with me: the good, the bad, the ugly. Now over forty-five years since graduation, our friendships are growing stronger than ever through regular get-togethers. Having the long history with this group of friends, and having their acceptance of me despite my trials, continues to be a restorative component of my life today.

Over the years of our marriage, Kaycee and I have started and led recovery groups in our home church, and experienced the joy of seeing marriages, families, and lives transformed as people work a spiritual program of recovery. Helping others journey toward sobriety has been an important component of our married life together.

We visit with my mom who lives an hour or so away. She's in good health and good spirits. My mom struggles a bit because my brother just does not like me, because of all the twists and turns my life took. He just wants nothing to do with me. A sad lesson I learned is that some relationships won't be restored.

I am humbled by, and grateful to, all the people who opened their hearts, gave of their time, and made many sacrifices on my behalf because they love the Lord and trust in His power to heal broken lives, even one so seemingly destroyed beyond repair as mine. I am grateful to those whom I loved and hurt badly that found it in their hearts to forgive, and allow me back into their lives.

My story testifies to the truth that we must never give up on people, no matter how many times they fail or how long recovery takes. We must never underestimate the healing power of prayer and love in the hands of the Lord. We must never give up hope.

To use the phrase "it takes a village", it takes much more than a village to heal, restore, and recover a life so broken as mine was. My overwhelming desire was and is to live out my life as Walt. Every single person in my life is like a mirror, each one reflecting who I am to them: Walt, a dad, a husband, a grandpa, a man in the loving hands of Christ, a man fully restored even with a part or so missing. That's only cosmetic, it doesn't define me. I love my life thanks to all those friends who held my hand and walked with me on the twisted path until I was whole enough to walk on my own.

The late Dr. Dennis Guernsey said it best when he wrote this note on the inside cover of my Bible:

Walt,

How long the journey, how twisted the road. How tired you've been at times, weary, discouraged beyond description. But how faithful has God been through it all. I am deeply appreciative of the power of God's grace in your life and the special place those people we both love have forever in your life.

It's still day by day.

Your friend in Christ
Dennis L. Kenny
August 1985

The most important thing I'd like you to remember is not me or my story, but the awesome truth that Jesus heals. No matter what the issue, or how badly broken the life, it is possible. If someone has the desire to recover and puts himself into the loving supportive arms of Jesus Christ and a body of vibrant believers, people who love him, pray for him and hold him accountable. Then healing and restoration will come to that badly broken life. Never give up hope. Those who are broken can rejoice—and trade their sorrows for a joy-filled life with Christ, just like I did.

We are very thankful that this is a success story. A story of hope. And above all, a story of an all-loving Father and the amazing grace of His Son, Jesus.

Walt is aptly described as a "Trophy of God's Grace." And in the midst of life's journey, I was fortunate to find a friend for life.

—Dr. Roy Thompson

Chapter 16.

Reflection 2015

Now nearly 30 years sober, married 18 years and free of the transgender life, I live to serve Jesus Christ by helping other transgenders find their way back from the devastating surgery.

If you or someone you know is caught in the web of gender reassignment, have faith. Pray. Never give up. Live a sober life and seek sound psychological counseling.

Restoration happened for this transgender and that's proof that a new life in Christ is available for all who want it.

Chapter 17.

Thoughts on Ministering to "Scary" People

While I was writing this book, I talked with Pastor Jeff Farrar many times. It became very clear that his personal perspective, as pastor of the church that spiritually supported me, would be extremely valuable to other pastors, elders and church leaders. With that in mind, I asked him to share some insights.

By Jeff Farrar

Upon hearing Walt's story many have asked what principles we at the church used that could help other pastors and church leaders when encountering people in extraordinary situations. I refer to them as "scary" people not because they are "scary," but because their situations and experience are so outside of ours that they scare us. We simply do not know what to do with them. For many Christian leaders, anything outside of our experience makes us nervous; we measure ourselves on knowing what to do. To this day Walt encounters Christians, especially leaders, who when they hear his story, are frightened by him. This often results in their rejection, and even attack, out of lack of understanding and a need to protect their church and their world.

One danger in looking back over years of a journey in ministry is to put an overly positive spin on things. From this end of the story, it looks wonderful and our instincts and wisdom get magnified. The truth is that the great majority of the time, we were operating with no experience and little understanding of how things would turn out. We were scrambling to stay faithful to our call to lead and protect the church while struggling to engage Laura/Walt in love and truth. The dominant feeling was how uncertain the future was and how out of control everything looked to us. That isn't a comfortable feeling but we were convinced that ministry of the Spirit often looks and feels just like that.

So without minimizing how uncertain we often were, I will attempt to give an account of the beliefs that compelled us forward and how God used a "scary" person to accomplish His work in us individually and corporately. I offer this simply as the path we followed in trying to honor the Lord.

Establishing Ground Rules

At the end of our first meeting, Laura asked if I would be willing to regularly meet with her. I was acutely aware of how far over my head I was. I knew she wasn't too much for the Lord, just too much for me. I had a sense the Spirit was calling me to encourage her, but I had no idea what that might mean.

Painfully aware of how little I had to offer, I told her two things were necessary for me to be involved with her. First I had to have the freedom to be completely honest with her. I couldn't let my ignorance and inexperience or her fragility keep me from being open with my thoughts, counsel and questions. She didn't need to agree with me, but without honesty as the basis of our relationship. I couldn't be involved with integrity.

Secondly, my elders needed to know about her. My responsibility and my protection required that I be accountable to them. I asked her to trust me that I would only share as much as was required for them to understand what we were both dealing with. From her past experience, this was very frightening for Laura. Though I assured her that they could be trusted and their prayers were powerful, it put her in a position of great vulnerability. Looking back I can see that this was a much greater act of courage and trust on Laura's part than I realized at the time.

Our sessions together weren't centered on psychological counsel. That important piece was ongoing alongside our meetings. My goal was to encourage her toward the Lord, to move her ahead in:

- honesty before God in prayer
- biblically-based decision making
- accountability in her lifestyle decisions
- freedom to accept God's grace and tenderness.

Some Convictions that Compelled Us
Jesus' example obligated us to accept and reach out to Laura.

One day Jesus was hosting a lunch of certain "types" of people – "tax-gatherers and sinners." Mark emphasizes the fact that "there were many of them, and they were following Him" (Mark 2:15, New American Standard Bible). Some religious leaders were scandalized by this and asked the disciples how He could eat and drink with such people. Jesus' response is powerful. He says, "It is not those who are healthy who need a physician, but those who are sick; I did not come to call the righteous, but sinners" (Mark 2:17, New American Standard Bible).

When I looked around at our church, there weren't many people outside of our comfort zone. Laura came from a horrible, terrifying situation. The fact that she was a challenge was no reason not to engage and serve her.

The issues facing us weren't really about Laura but about what kind of a church we were.

Matthew 25 describes that the Lord judges us based on our treatment of hurting, needy people. The ones accepted are those of whom Jesus says "For I was hungry, and you gave Me something to eat; I was thirsty, and you gave Me drink; I was a stranger, and you invited Me in; naked and you clothed Me; I was sick and you visited Me; I was in prison, and you came to Me" (Matthew 25:35, 36, NASB). It is fascinating that those called to meet His needs never saw Him. Jesus' answer is "that the extent that you did it (or did not do it) to one of these brothers of Mine, even the least of them, you did it (or did not do it) to Me" (Matthew 25:40, 45, NASB).

I believe the Spirit was inviting us into a new level of obedience and trust. I had some sense that how we dealt with

Laura would determine the type of leaders and the type of church we would be. We had talked (even bragged) about being a community of grace, yet here was a person whose need forced us to either live that out in the midst of uncertainty and trust, or choose safety and pass her by.

Our call was to obey the Lord in ministry and not preserve the status quo or avoid criticism.

Pastors and elders are rightly aware of protecting the church. Yet it is a small step from proper concern for the good of the church to protecting our reputation as leaders and avoiding criticism. It is clear from Jesus' model that His character was defamed due to His commitment to loving needy, even "scary" people. Jesus defends His choices to fellowship with these people and recounts how His enemies tried to use it against Him. "The Son of Man has come eating and drinking; and you say, 'Behold, a gluttonous man, and a drunkard, a friend of tax-gatherers and sinners'" (Luke 7:34, NASB). They didn't say these things because Jesus ate too much food and drank too much wine. It was because of those He spent time with and shared meals with.

We were aware that many would just not understand why we would welcome a person like Laura in our church. We discussed the fact that if Laura became visible, some might even leave the church. After thinking this through, our conclusion was that those individuals probably needed to leave the church and find a place that would better suit them. There was much more at stake here than simply keeping attendance numbers up.

Laura was hurting and broken before the Lord, not rebellious or defiant.

This became the determining factor in how we responded to people in need. I often probed Laura and asked the Lord for insight into her heart. There is a world of difference between a broken person and a defiant person. Someone who has failed and is weak and hurting needs to be encouraged, lifted up, gently pointed to the truth and urged to trust the Lord. A defiant person needs to be exhorted, confronted, even opposed by the weight of Scripture in the hope of pulling then back to obedience.

While Laura's past choices were, by her own admission, at best foolish and destructive, her longing to honor God in the midst of her pain and willingness to follow the truth were apparent. She wasn't a person defiantly shaking her fist at God claiming she had the right to do whatever she wanted. She was crushed and bowed before God seeking His will in the midst of the mess her life had become. Whether we understood her situation or not, it was her heart that obligated us to engage her in love and support.

As Laura became part of the church, we who knew her past were sometimes faced with tough ethical choices. When would protecting her "secret" compromise us? I don't know that we always made the wisest decisions. There were times we had to face the ones who were kept in the dark for Laura's protection who felt betrayed when they discovered the whole story. In those painful moments, we were compelled to shelter Laura/Walt from even knowing those things were occurring. Deciding to do what we as elders believed was biblically correct certainly didn't exempt us from difficult times and some painful encounters.

How Far God Has Brought Us

It was a blazing hot day as Walt and I stood together before Roy Thompson in his backyard. He was the groom and I was the best man. Next to Walt was a beautiful, glowing Kaycee. A group of family and friends had gathered to witness their wedding.

As I stood there looking at Walt, I remembered another scene. It was Easter dinner, shortly after Laura had come into our lives. I was looking out from my kitchen to the living room. There on the couch were my ninety-year-old grandmother, my mom, and Laura, all dressed up for Easter, sitting on the couch chatting, as our three kids played with my dad on the floor.

Susan, my wife, and I were in the kitchen preparing food. We looked at each other, and began to giggle. Our extended family knew nothing about Laura other than that she was a friend. We were convinced that sharing our family with Laura was absolutely the correct thing to do. Yet we were struck by how following the Lord had put us in such an unusual circumstance. We were in no way ashamed of Laura. In fact, we were proud of the steps she had taken and the growth we could see. Yet we had no idea how Laura's life would unfold. All we knew was the Lord was at work.

Standing in the Thompson's backyard years later, seeing Walt and Kaycee hold hands and commit their lives to each other before the Lord, I was struck by God's goodness and faithfulness to all of us. I felt overwhelmed at the privilege of having witnessed God's miraculous power in creating a trophy of grace.

More information

More information about this radical treatment procedure can be found at:

www.SexChangeRegret.com
Essential information and stories about sex change regret. Over 100,000 people a year visit the website from around the world and many contact Walt for individual guidance.

Walt Heyer's blog at www.waltheyer.com
Current news and information about sex change regret.

Contact the author

Contact the author at waltsbook@yahoo.com

More Books by Walt Heyer

Gender, Lies and Suicide
A Whistleblower Speaks Out

Transgenders undergo hormone injections and irreversible surgeries in a desperate effort to feel better, yet they attempt and commit suicide at an alarming rate, even after treatment. Walt digs into the issues behind transgender suicide and shares some heart-wrenching letters from those who regret the decision to change genders.

Paper Genders
Pulling the Mask off the Transgender Phenomenon

A fresh perspective on the medical treatment for gender identity issues, combining well-researched facts with personal accounts. Exposes and debunks the promises of gender change surgery and shines a light on the suicides and dissatisfaction that the advocates would prefer to keep hidden.

"The research, reason, passion (even outrage) and compassion makes for compelling reading."

Perfected With Love
A powerful and inspiring true story

One church says "No" to a scary person. Another church says "Yes" and the astonishing results demonstrate why Scripture says of faith, hope and love that "the greatest of these is love." This inspiring true story will encourage and equip you and your church with ways to show God's love to a transgender person.

Available at www.SexChangeRegret.com, Amazon.com, and Barnes and Noble.